This Copy of

THE
FOCUSED STOIC
JOURNAL

Belongs to:

_____

INDEX pt I

Page(s)

18	Key
20	
21	
22	Set Your Goals
23	Value Brainstorming
24	Stoic Virtues
25	Your Top 5 Values
26	
27	
28	Personal SWOT Analysis - Strengths
30	Personal SWOT Analysis - Weaknesses
32	Personal SWOT Analysis - Threats
34	Personal SWOT Analysis - Opportunities
36	
37	
38	Goal Setting Exercises
40	Goal Setting Your Preferred Results
42	One Year Goal 1
44	One Year Goal 2
46	One Year Goal 3
48	One Year Goal 4
50	
51	
52	Quarterly Goal Setting

Page(s)

54	28 Day Goal Setting - Weeks 1-4
55	7 Day Goal Setting - Week 1
56	Weekly Theme
57	Weekly Reflection
58	
59	
60	28 Day Calendar - Weeks 1-4
62	Week 1 Planner
64	
65	
66	Sunday - Week 1, Day 1 - Morning Preparation
68	Sunday - Week 1, Day 1 - Evening Review
70	Monday - Week 1, Day 2 - Morning Preparation
72	Monday - Week 1, Day 2 - Evening Review
74	Tuesday - Week 1, Day 3 - Morning Preparation
76	Tuesday - Week 1, Day 3 - Evening Review
78	Wednesday - Week 1, Day 4 - Morning Preparation
80	Wednesday - Week 1, Day 4 - Evening Review
82	Thursday - Week 1, Day 5 - Morning Preparation
84	Thursday - Week 1, Day 5 - Evening Review
86	Friday - Week 1, Day 6 - Morning Preparation
88	Friday - Week 1, Day 6 - Evening Review
90	Saturday - Week 1, Day 7 - Morning Preparation
92	Saturday - Week 1, Day 7 - Evening Review
94	
95	

cont'd

INDEX pt II

Page(s)

96	Week 1 Gratitude Log
98	Weekly Premeditation of Obstacles
100	Week 1 Review
101	7 Day Goal Setting - Week 2
102	
103	Mandala
104	Weekly Theme
105	Weekly Reflection
106	
107	
108	Week 2 Planner
110	Sunday - Week 2, Day 1 - Morning Preparation
112	Sunday - Week 2, Day 1 - Evening Review
114	Monday - Week 2, Day 2 - Morning Preparation
116	Monday - Week 2, Day 2 - Evening Review
118	Tuesday - Week 2, Day 3 - Morning Preparation
120	Tuesday - Week 2, Day 3 - Evening Review
122	Wednesday - Week 2, Day 4 - Morning Preparation
124	Wednesday - Week 2, Day 4 - Evening Review
126	Thursday - Week 2, Day 5 - Morning Preparation
128	Thursday - Week 2, Day 5 - Evening Review
130	Friday - Week 2, Day 6 - Morning Preparation
132	Friday - Week 2, Day 6 - Evening Review
134	Saturday - Week 2, Day 7 - Morning Preparation

Page(s)	
136	Saturday - Week 2, Day 7 - Evening Review
138	
139	
140	Week 2 Gratitude Log
142	Weekly Premeditation of Obstacles
144	Week 2 Review
145	7 Day Goal Setting - Week 3
146	
147	Mandala
148	Weekly Theme
149	Weekly Reflection
150	
151	
152	Week 3 Planner
154	Sunday - Week 3, Day 1 - Morning Preparation
156	Sunday - Week 3, Day 1 - Evening Review
158	Monday - Week 3, Day 2 - Morning Preparation
160	Monday - Week 3, Day 2 - Evening Review
162	Tuesday - Week 3, Day 3 - Morning Preparation
164	Tuesday - Week 3, Day 3 - Evening Review
166	Wednesday - Week 3, Day 4 - Morning Preparation
168	Wednesday - Week 3, Day 4 - Evening Review
170	Thursday - Week 3, Day 5 - Morning Preparation
172	Thursday - Week 3, Day 5 - Evening Review
174	Friday - Week 3, Day 6 - Morning Preparation
176	Friday - Week 3, Day 6 - Evening Review

cont'd

INDEX pt III

Page(s)

178	Saturday - Week 3, Day 7 - Morning Preparation
180	Saturday - Week 3, Day 7 - Evening Review
182	
183	
184	Week 3 Gratitude Log
186	Weekly Premeditation of Obstacles
188	Week 3 Review
189	7 Day Goal Setting - Week 4
190	
191	Mandala
192	Weekly Theme
193	Weekly Reflection
194	
195	
196	Week 4 Planner
198	Sunday - Week 4, Day 1 - Morning Preparation
200	Sunday - Week 4, Day 1 - Evening Review
202	Monday - Week 4, Day 2 - Morning Preparation
204	Monday - Week 4, Day 2 - Evening Review
206	Tuesday - Week 4, Day 3 - Morning Preparation
208	Tuesday - Week 4, Day 3 - Evening Review
210	Wednesday - Week 4, Day 4 - Morning Preparation
212	Wednesday - Week 4, Day 4 - Evening Review
214	Thursday - Week 4, Day 5 - Morning Preparation

Page(s)	
216	Thursday - Week 4, Day 5 - Evening Review
218	Friday - Week 4, Day 6 - Morning Preparation
220	Friday - Week 4, Day 6 - Evening Review
222	Saturday - Week 4, Day 7 - Morning Preparation
224	Saturday - Week 4, Day 7 - Evening Review
226	
227	
228	Week 4 Gratitude Log
230	Weekly Premeditation of Obstacles
232	28 Day Tracking Weeks 1-4
234	Health & Wellness Review - Weeks 1-4
236	Week 4 Review
237	28 Day Review - Weeks 1-4
238	28 Day Goal Setting - Weeks 5-8
239	7 Day Goal Setting - Week 5
240	
241	Mandala
242	Weekly Theme
243	Weekly Reflection
244	
245	
246	28 Day Calendar - Weeks 5-8
248	Week 5 Planner
250	Sunday - Week 5, Day 1 - Morning Preparation
252	Sunday - Week 5, Day 1 - Evening Review
254	Monday - Week 5, Day 2 - Morning Preparation

cont'd

INDEX pt IV

Page(s)

256	Monday - Week 5, Day 2 - Evening Review
258	Tuesday - Week 5, Day 3 - Morning Preparation
260	Tuesday - Week 5, Day 3 - Evening Review
262	Wednesday - Week 5, Day 4 - Morning Preparation
264	Wednesday - Week 5, Day 4 - Evening Review
266	Thursday - Week 5, Day 5 - Morning Preparation
268	Thursday - Week 5, Day 5 - Evening Review
270	Friday - Week 5, Day 6 - Morning Preparation
272	Friday - Week 5, Day 6 - Evening Review
274	Saturday - Week 5, Day 7 - Morning Preparation
276	Saturday - Week 5, Day 7 - Evening Review
278	
279	
280	Week 5 Gratitude Log
282	Weekly Premeditation of Obstacles
284	Week 5 Review
285	7 Day Goal Setting - Week 6
286	
287	Mandala
288	Weekly Theme
289	Weekly Reflection
290	
291	
292	Week 6 Planner

Page(s)

294	Sunday - Week 6, Day 1 - Morning Preparation
296	Sunday - Week 6, Day 1 - Evening Review
298	Monday - Week 6, Day 2 - Morning Preparation
300	Monday - Week 6, Day 2 - Evening Review
302	Tuesday - Week 6, Day 3 - Morning Preparation
304	Tuesday - Week 6, Day 3 - Evening Review
306	Wednesday - Week 6, Day 4 - Morning Preparation
308	Wednesday - Week 6, Day 4 - Evening Review
310	Thursday - Week 6, Day 5 - Morning Preparation
312	Thursday - Week 6, Day 5 - Evening Review
314	Friday - Week 6, Day 6 - Morning Preparation
316	Friday - Week 6, Day 6 - Evening Review
318	Saturday - Week 6, Day 7 - Morning Preparation
320	Saturday - Week 6, Day 7 - Evening Review
322	
323	
324	Week 6 Gratitude Log
326	Weekly Premeditation of Obstacles
328	Week 6 Review
329	7 Day Goal Setting - Week 7
330	
331	Mandala
332	Weekly Theme
333	Weekly Reflection
334	
335	

cont'd

INDEX pt V

Page(s)

336	Week 7 Planner
338	Sunday - Week 7, Day 1 - Morning Preparation
340	Sunday - Week 7, Day 1 - Evening Review
342	Monday - Week 7, Day 2 - Morning Preparation
344	Monday - Week 7, Day 2 - Evening Review
346	Tuesday - Week 7, Day 3 - Morning Preparation
348	Tuesday - Week 7, Day 3 - Evening Review
350	Wednesday - Week 7, Day 4 - Morning Preparation
352	Wednesday - Week 7, Day 4 - Evening Review
354	Thursday - Week 7, Day 5 - Morning Preparation
356	Thursday - Week 7, Day 5 - Evening Review
358	Friday - Week 7, Day 6 - Morning Preparation
360	Friday - Week 7, Day 6 - Evening Review
362	Saturday - Week 7, Day 7 - Morning Preparation
364	Saturday - Week 7, Day 7 - Evening Review
366	
367	
368	Week 7 Gratitude Log
370	Momento Mori Reflection
372	Week 7 Review
373	7 Day Goal Setting - Week 8
374	
375	Mandala
376	Weekly Theme

Page(s)

377	Weekly Reflection
378	
379	
380	Week 8 Planner
382	Sunday - Week 8, Day 1 - Morning Preparation
384	Sunday - Week 8, Day 1 - Evening Review
386	Monday - Week 8, Day 2 - Morning Preparation
388	Monday - Week 8, Day 2 - Evening Review
390	Tuesday - Week 8, Day 3 - Morning Preparation
392	Tuesday - Week 8, Day 3 - Evening Review
394	Wednesday - Week 8, Day 4 - Morning Preparation
396	Wednesday - Week 8, Day 4 - Evening Review
398	Thursday - Week 8, Day 5 - Morning Preparation
400	Thursday - Week 8, Day 5 - Evening Review
402	Friday - Week 8, Day 6 - Morning Preparation
404	Friday - Week 8, Day 6 - Evening Review
406	Saturday - Week 8, Day 7 - Morning Preparation
408	Saturday - Week 8, Day 7 - Evening Review
410	
411	
412	Week 8 Gratitude Log
414	Weekly Premeditation of Obstacles
416	28 Day Tracking Weeks 5-8
418	Health & Wellness Review - Weeks 5-8
420	Week 8 Review
421	28 Day Review - Weeks 5-8

cont'd

INDEX pt VI

Page(s)

422	35 Day Goal Setting - Weeks 9-13
423	7 Day Goal Setting - Week 9
424	
425	Mandala
426	Weekly Theme
427	Weekly Reflection
428	
429	
430	35 Day Calendar - Weeks 9-13
432	Week 9 Planner
434	Sunday - Week 9, Day 1 - Morning Preparation
436	Sunday - Week 9, Day 1 - Evening Review
438	Monday - Week 9, Day 2 - Morning Preparation
440	Monday - Week 9, Day 2 - Evening Review
442	Tuesday - Week 9, Day 3 - Morning Preparation
444	Tuesday - Week 9, Day 3 - Evening Review
446	Wednesday - Week 9, Day 4 - Morning Preparation
448	Wednesday - Week 9, Day 4 - Evening Review
450	Thursday - Week 9, Day 5 - Morning Preparation
452	Thursday - Week 9, Day 5 - Evening Review
454	Friday - Week 9, Day 6 - Morning Preparation
456	Friday - Week 9, Day 6 - Evening Review
458	Saturday - Week 9, Day 7 - Morning Preparation
460	Saturday - Week 9, Day 7 - Evening Review

Page(s)	
462	
463	
464	Week 9 Gratitude Log
466	Weekly Premeditation of Obstacles
468	Week 9 Review
469	7 Day Goal Setting - Week 10
470	
471	Mandala
472	Weekly Theme
473	Weekly Reflection
474	
475	
476	Week 10 Planner
478	Sunday - Week 10, Day 1 - Morning Preparation
480	Sunday - Week 10, Day 1 - Evening Review
482	Monday - Week 10, Day 2 - Morning Preparation
484	Monday - Week 10, Day 2 - Evening Review
486	Tuesday - Week 10, Day 3 - Morning Preparation
488	Tuesday - Week 10, Day 3 - Evening Review
490	Wednesday - Week 10, Day 4 - Morning Preparation
492	Wednesday - Week 10, Day 4 - Evening Review
494	Thursday - Week 10, Day 5 - Morning Preparation
496	Thursday - Week 10, Day 5 - Evening Review
498	Friday - Week 10, Day 6 - Morning Preparation
500	Friday - Week 10, Day 6 - Evening Review
502	Saturday - Week 10, Day 7 - Morning Preparation

cont'd

INDEX pt VII

Page(s)

504	Saturday - Week 10, Day 7 - Evening Review
506	
507	
508	Week 10 Gratitude Log
510	Weekly Premeditation of Obstacles
512	Week 10 Review
513	7 Day Goal Setting - Week 11
514	
515	Mandala
516	Weekly Theme
517	Weekly Reflection
518	
519	
520	Week 11 Planner
522	Sunday - Week 11, Day 1 - Morning Preparation
524	Sunday - Week 11, Day 1 - Evening Review
526	Monday - Week 11, Day 2 - Morning Preparation
528	Monday - Week 11, Day 2 - Evening Review
530	Tuesday - Week 11, Day 3 - Morning Preparation
532	Tuesday - Week 11, Day 3 - Evening Review
534	Wednesday - Week 11, Day 4 - Morning Preparation
536	Wednesday - Week 11, Day 4 - Evening Review
538	Thursday - Week 11, Day 5 - Morning Preparation
540	Thursday - Week 11, Day 5 - Evening Review

Page(s)	
542	Friday - Week 11, Day 6 - Morning Preparation
544	Friday - Week 11, Day 6 - Evening Review
546	Saturday - Week 11, Day 7 - Morning Preparation
548	Saturday - Week 11, Day 7 - Evening Review
550	
551	
552	Week 11 Gratitude Log
554	Weekly Premeditation of Obstacles
556	Week 11 Review
557	7 Day Goal Setting - Week 12
558	
559	Mandala
560	Weekly Theme
561	Weekly Reflection
562	
563	
564	Week 12 Planner
566	Sunday - Week 12, Day 1 - Morning Preparation
568	Sunday - Week 12, Day 1 - Evening Review
570	Monday - Week 12, Day 2 - Morning Preparation
572	Monday - Week 12, Day 2 - Evening Review
574	Tuesday - Week 12, Day 3 - Morning Preparation
576	Tuesday - Week 12, Day 3 - Evening Review
578	Wednesday - Week 12, Day 4 - Morning Preparation
580	Wednesday - Week 12, Day 4 - Evening Review
582	Thursday - Week 12, Day 5 - Morning Preparation

cont'd

INDEX pt VIII

Page(s)

584	Thursday - Week 12, Day 5 - Evening Review
586	Friday - Week 12, Day 6 - Morning Preparation
588	Friday - Week 12, Day 6 - Evening Review
590	Saturday - Week 12, Day 7 - Morning Preparation
592	Saturday - Week 12, Day 7 - Evening Review
594	
595	
596	Week 12 Gratitude Log
598	Weekly Premeditation of Obstacles
600	28 Day Tracking Weeks 9-12
602	Week 12 Review
603	7 Day Goal Setting - Week 13
604	
605	Mandala
606	Weekly Theme
607	Weekly Reflection
608	
609	
610	Week 13 Planner
612	Sunday - Week 13, Day 1 - Morning Preparation
614	Sunday - Week 13, Day 1 - Evening Review
616	Monday - Week 13, Day 2 - Morning Preparation
618	Monday - Week 13, Day 2 - Evening Review
620	Tuesday - Week 13, Day 3 - Morning Preparation

Page(s)

622	Tuesday - Week 13, Day 3 - Evening Review
624	Wednesday - Week 13, Day 4 - Morning Preparation
626	Wednesday - Week 13, Day 4 - Evening Review
628	Thursday - Week 13, Day 5 - Morning Preparation
630	Thursday - Week 13, Day 5 - Evening Review
632	Friday - Week 13, Day 6 - Morning Preparation
634	Friday - Week 13, Day 6 - Evening Review
636	Saturday - Week 13, Day 7 - Morning Preparation
638	Saturday - Week 13, Day 7 - Evening Review
640	
641	
642	Week 13 Gratitude Log
644	Weekly Premeditation of Obstacles
646	7 Day Tracking Week 13
647	
648	Health & Wellness Review - Weeks 9-13
650	Week 13 Review
651	35 Day Review - Weeks 9-13
652	Quarterly Review
654	
655	Mandala
656	Writing & Gratitude Prompts
658	Morning & Evening Meditation Sequences
660	Zazen & Panta Rhei Guided Meditations
662	Gratitude & Adversity Guided Meditations
664	Forgiveness & Agape Guided Meditations

KEY

If you are using symbols, record them here for easy reference.

20

SET YOUR GOALS

If one does not know to which port one is sailing, no wind is favourable.
— Seneca

*** If you have already done the one year and quarterly goal setting in the last year in a previous Focused Stoic Journal, you can skip this until a year has passed unless you feel it would benefit you to repeat it. ***

Over the next few pages you will work on setting the goals you want to achieve during the next 91 days while you work on this journal. You will:

1. Define your values

2. Do a personal SWOT Analysis (Strengths, Weaknesses, Opportunities, and Threats)

A SWOT is an important step in goal setting as it shows us which strengths and opportunities can help us in attaining a goal, and which weaknesses and threats will be in the way. It also helps us pick goals that can promote our strengths, reduce weaknesses, exploit the opportunities and develop plans to minimize threats.

3. Brainstorm on what you would like to see in your ideal future - general goals, dreams, what you would like to achieve, to have, to do or experience.

4. Prioritize your goals based on what is most important and achievable.

6. Break your goals down by long term and short term goals.

7. Set your 91 day goals. Then break them down into your first 28 and 7 day goals.

VALUE BRAINSTORMING

This is to increase awareness of what really matters to you by identifying your top five life values. What's most important in your life? You can't know how to live your best life if you don't examine what is truly best.

Take a few minutes to brainstorm what your own values are. Try not to reference the list on the next page. But if you have difficulty, then you should refer to the next page.

Review the list of Stoic virtues and values on the next page and compare.

STOIC VIRTUES

Common values and how they can be oriented with Stoic Virtues

PRUDENCE

- Wisdom
- Reason
- Open Mindedness
- Appropriate caution
- Knowing good from bad
- Good Counsel
- Good Calculation
- Good Understanding
- Resourcefulness
- Inquisitiveness
- Truthfulness
- Decisiveness
- Discretion
- *Prosoche*/ Attentiveness
- Consideration
- Purpose
- Creativity
- Beauty
- Harmony
- Precision
- Gratitude
- Preparedness
- Foresight
- Knowledge

MORALITY

- *Sympatheia*
- Philanthropy
- Mutual Benefit
- Benevolence
- Compassion
- Cooperation
- Generosity
- Helpfulness
- *Agape*
- Tactfulness
- Altruism
- Kindness
- Equity
- Cosmopolitanism
- Fairness
- Honesty
- Piety
- Duty
- Justice
- Reciprocity
- Charity
- Courtesy
- Impartial Judgement

TEMPERENCE

- Decorum
- Self-Control
- Moderation
- Patience
- Humility
- Frugality
- Dignity
- Clemency/ Forgiveness
- Impartial Judgement
- Seemliness
- Modesty
- Peacefulness
- Forebearance
- Good Discipline
- Chastity
- Orderliness
- Tolerance
- Abstemity
- Cleanliness
- Thrift
- Austerity
- Detachment
- Conciseness
- Flexibility
- Equanimity
- Docility
- Realism

FORTITUDE

- Courage
- Endurance
- Confidence
- Cheerfulness
- Determination
- Tenacity
- Love of Duty
- Commitment
- Stalwartness
- Perseverence
- Contentment
- Steadfastness
- Industriousness
- High-Mindedness
- Trustworthiness
- Integrity
- Responsibility
- Assertiveness
- Sincerity
- Diligence
- Prowess
- Loyalty
- Skillfulness
- Stewardship
- Self-Reliance

YOUR TOP FIVE VALUES

Prioritize the top five of your most important values. List them here. With each value, write what that value means to you personally, and why it is important to you.

Value 1

Means to me

It is important to me because

Value 2

Means to me

It is important to me because

Value 3

Means to me

It is important to me because

Value 4

Means to me

It is important to me because

Value 5

Means to me

It is important to me because

27

PERSONAL SWOT ANALYSIS
STRENGTHS

What would you or others say are your positive habits and traits?

What would you or others say comes most easily to you?

What skills have you trained to develop?

What would you or others say you do best?

What would you or others say are your values which you best embody?

What would you or others say are your greatest achievements?

What would you or others say are aspects that are positive and unique about you?

What would you or others say are resources available to you?

With which activities do you experience flow? When does your time fly by? What are some things you could spend hours actively doing?

What parts of your current life brings you the most pride?

What do you enjoy doing most?

PERSONAL SWOT ANALYSIS
WEAKNESSES

What would you or others say are your negative habits and traits?

What tasks do you avoid doing because of a lack of confidence?

What tasks do you avoid because you dislike doing them?

Where would you or others say you are struggling the most in life?

What would you or others say are your values which you least embody?

What fears do you have that may be holding you back?

What disadvantages do you have (education, skills, networks, etc.)?

What would you or others say are resources you are lacking?

What would you or others say are parts of your training or education which need improvement?

What parts of your life do you try to hide away from others due to feeling ashamed of them?

PERSONAL SWOT ANALYSIS
THREATS

What obstacles do you face?

What new developments could hurt or impede you?

What opponents are acting against you?

Which is the biggest external danger you see?

What are the biggest risks you are facing?

Could any of your weaknesses prevent you from succeeding?

Could any of your strengths hold you back?

Do you have any obligations (work or otherwise) that may limit your development?

Which of your weaknesses increase the risk from any threats, and how?

What other threats you can see?

PERSONAL SWOT ANALYSIS
OPPORTUNITIES

Which of your values might help you reach your goals?

Is there a need for what you do well that others aren't fulfilling well?

What new developments can you use to your advantage?

Are you competitors or opponents failing somewhere?

What could you do that isn't being done by anyone else well enough?

How can you turn the threats into an opportunity?

Which strengths can help reduce the risk from your threats, and how?

Which of your weaknesses could you turn into strengths or opportunities, and how?

What activities do you: 1. Enjoy doing 2. Do well 3. Get into a state of flow 4. Do to benefit others 5. Have an ability to make an income doing?

What are other opportunities you can see?

36

GOAL SETTING EXERCISES

These exercises are designed to help you begin to imagine what your ideal future could look like. Answer the questions with anything that comes to mind without judging the thoughts or writing. It can be a raw stream of consciousness.

If there were one and only one thing you could do better, what would you want it to be?

What could you do with your spare time that would be both highly productive and pleasant for you?

If you could have any job that you think you would excel at, what would that job look like? Why would you like it?

What do you want to learn more about?

List 3-5 habits you would like to improve.

If you could handpick your friends, what kind of friends would you pick?

If you could have exactly the family life that you wanted, what would that look like?

GOAL SETTING YOUR PREFERRED RESULTS

With the past exercises in mind, brainstorm anything you would like to have, accomplish, give, do, create, or experience between now and 20 years from now. Write anything that is in your thoughts of what you would like. There are no wrong ideas. The results you want can either be about your own character, or an external result that you would prefer. Leave a space on each side for some numbers.

Now go over what you have written. On the right of each result write the minimum amount of time you think you could realistically achieve the dream; 1/4, 1/2, 1, 3, 5, 10, or 20+ years. On the left of each idea number each idea in order of which are most important to you.

○ Compare your preferred results and your chosen values.
Cross out any result that contradicts your values.
Checkmark any result that is well aligned with your values

○ For any results that you expect would take longer than 1 year to accomplish, add another goal which you would need to accomplish in just 1 year to move towards that longer term result.

○ Make your one year goals SMART -
Specific, Measurable, Attainable, Realistic, Time-bound
Strike out any goal that is not realistically attainable in a year.
Change any vague goals to a specific and measurable result

Review your list and choose your top 4 one-year goals. Then break down your one-year goals to 4 quarterly milestones. What do you need to accomplish by the end of each quarter to meet your goal?

GOAL 1:

Quarterly Goals

Q1	Q2
Q3	Q4

GOAL 2:

Quarterly Goals

Q1	Q2
Q3	Q4

GOAL 3:

Quarterly Goals

Q1	Q2
Q3	Q4

GOAL 4:

Quarterly Goals

Q1	Q2
Q3	Q4

ONE YEAR GOAL 1

Do you want this result mainly for yourself, for others, or both?

How would you benefit if you achieve this goal?

How would your family and friends benefit?

How would your community benefit?

What do you expect would be worse if you moved farther away from this goal?

In what ways does this goal align with your own values?

How would achieving this change your view of yourself?

What parts of just working towards this goal would you find satisfying, even before it is accomplished?

How would you feel to be lying on your deathbed one day knowing you had not attempted this?

What other reasons do you have to prefer this result?

ONE YEAR GOAL 2

Do you want this result mainly for yourself, for others, or both?

How would you benefit if you achieve this goal?

How would your family and friends benefit?

How would your community benefit?

What do you expect would be worse if you moved farther away from this goal?

In what ways does this goal align with your own values?

How would achieving this change your view of yourself?

What parts of just working towards this goal would you find satisfying, even before it is accomplished?

How would you feel to be lying on your deathbed one day knowing you had not attempted this?

What other reasons do you have to prefer this result?

ONE YEAR GOAL 3

Do you want this result mainly for yourself, for others, or both?

How would you benefit if you achieve this goal?

How would your family and friends benefit?

How would your community benefit?

What do you expect would be worse if you moved farther away from this goal?

In what ways does this goal align with your own values?

How would achieving this change your view of yourself?

What parts of just working towards this goal would you find satisfying, even before it is accomplished?

How would you feel to be lying on your deathbed one day knowing you had not attempted this?

What other reasons do you have to prefer this result?

ONE YEAR GOAL 4

Do you want this result mainly for yourself, for others, or both?

How would you benefit if you achieve this goal?

How would your family and friends benefit?

How would your community benefit?

What do you expect would be worse if you moved farther away from this goal?

In what ways does this goal align with your own values?

How would achieving this change your view of yourself?

What parts of just working towards this goal would you find satisfying, even before it is accomplished?

How would you feel to be lying on your deathbed one day knowing you had not attempted this?

What other reasons do you have to prefer this result?

50

QUARTERLY GOAL SETTING

Review your 1 year goals. Look at the steps you should do to achieve the goals, and what you can do to reduce the chances of the obstacles you anticipated. With those in mind, what are your goals for the next 91 days? Make them specific and achievable in 91 days.

What are the steps to take to most likely achieve the goals?

What are some likely preferred results if the goals are met?

What are some likely unpreferred results if the goals are not met?

What are some obstacles that may obstruct meeting the goal?

What can you do to prepare for or reduce the chances of them happening?

What should you do if these obstacles happen?

28-DAY GOAL SETTING - WEEKS 1-4

Review pages 42 & 43. Consider the steps you should do to achieve your quarterly goals, and what you can do to reduce the chances of the obstacles you anticipated. With those in mind, what are your goals for the next 28 days? Make them specific and achievable in 28 days.

What are some obstacles you are likely to face with these goals?

What should you do if these obstacles happen?

What can you do to prepare for or reduce the chances of them happening?

7-DAY GOAL SETTING - WEEK 1

Break down your 28 day goals. Consider the steps you should do to achieve the goals, and what you can do to reduce the chances of the obstacles you anticipated. With those in mind, what are your goals for the next 7 days? Make them specific and achievable in 7 days.

Why are these steps important?

What part of these steps are in your control?

WEEKLY THEME

Live According to Truth & Reason

WEEKLY REFLECTION

(See pg 656 for writing prompts)

28 DAY CALENDAR - WEEKS 1-4

	SUNDAY	MONDAY	TUESDAY
WEEK 1			
WEEK 2			
WEEK 3			
WEEK 4			

WEDNESDAY	THURSDAY	FRIDAY	SATURDAY

WEEK 1 PLANNER

	SUNDAY	MONDAY	TUESDAY

	WEDNESDAY	THURSDAY	FRIDAY	SATURDAY

SUNDAY — MORNING PREPARATION
WEEK 1, DAY 1

DATE:

How long did you sleep?   Meditate ☐ (pg 658)

How well did you sleep? /5   Exercise ☐

Morning Reading:

NOTES:

Review your 7-day goals. With those goals in mind, make a **'Knockout List'** of 3-5 tasks you must work to complete today. Specify the tasks, and make them something you expect you can achieve today.

What are some obstacles you are likely to face today?

What can you do to prepare for or reduce the chances of them happening?

What should you do if these obstacles happen?

> "Truth is the beginning of every good to the gods, and of every good to man."
> — *Plato*

(See pg 656 for writing prompts)

EVENING REVIEW

BREAKFAST	LUNCH	SUPPER	SNACKS

What were the most significant obstacles you faced today?

How could these obstacles have been worse?

How did you or how can you mitigate these obstacles?

How can you reduce the chances of them reoccurring?

How can these obstacles benefit you?

What mistakes did you make today?

What could you have done that would have been worse?

What can you do to mitigate these mistakes?

What could you do better next time?

What did you do well today?

What can you look forward to tomorrow?

Did you do what was appropriate to complete your tasks?	YES / NO
Did you complete your knockout list?	YES / NO
Are you closer to your goals today?	YES / NO
Did you behave according to your principles?	YES / NO

Fill in your Gratitude Log and 28 Day Tracking

Evening Reading:

Meditate ☐
(pg 659)

MONDAY
MORNING PREPARATION
WEEK 1, DAY 2

DATE:

How long did you sleep?   Meditate ☐ (pg 658)

How well did you sleep? /5   Exercise ☐

Morning Reading:

NOTES:

Review your 7-day goals. With those goals in mind, make a **'Knockout List'** of 3-5 tasks you must work to complete today. Specify the tasks, and make them something you expect you can achieve today.

What are some obstacles you are likely to face today?

What can you do to prepare for or reduce the chances of them happening?

What should you do if these obstacles happen?

> "If a man would pursue Philosophy, his first task is to throw away conceit. For it is impossible for a man to begin to learn what he has a conceit that he already knows."
>
> *- Epictetus*

(See pg 656 for writing prompts)

EVENING REVIEW

BREAKFAST	LUNCH	SUPPER	SNACKS

What were the most significant obstacles you faced today?

How could these obstacles have been worse?

How did you or how can you mitigate these obstacles?

How can you reduce the chances of them reoccurring?

How can these obstacles benefit you?

What mistakes did you make today?

What could you have done that would have been worse?

What can you do to mitigate these mistakes?

What could you do better next time?

What did you do well today?

What can you look forward to tomorrow?

Did you do what was appropriate to complete your tasks?	**YES / NO**
Did you complete your knockout list?	**YES / NO**
Are you closer to your goals today?	**YES / NO**
Did you behave according to your principles?	**YES / NO**

Fill in your Gratitude Log and 28 Day Tracking

Evening Reading:

Meditate ☐
(pg 659)

TUESDAY — MORNING PREPARATION
WEEK 1, DAY 3

DATE:

How long did you sleep? Meditate ☐ Morning Reading:
(pg 658)

How well did you sleep? /5 Exercise ☐

NOTES:

Review your 7-day goals. With those goals in mind, make a **'Knockout List'** of 3-5 tasks you must work to complete today. Specify the tasks, and make them something you expect you can achieve today.

What are some obstacles you are likely to face today?

What can you do to prepare for or reduce the chances of them happening?

What should you do if these obstacles happen?

> "Men are apt to mistake the strength of their feeling for the strength of their argument. The heated mind resents the chill touch and relentless scrutiny of logic."
> — *William Gladstone*

(See pg 656 for writing prompts)

EVENING REVIEW

BREAKFAST	LUNCH	SUPPER	SNACKS

What were the most significant obstacles you faced today?

How could these obstacles have been worse?

How did you or how can you mitigate these obstacles?

How can you reduce the chances of them reoccurring?

How can these obstacles benefit you?

What mistakes did you make today?

What could you have done that would have been worse?

What can you do to mitigate these mistakes?

What could you do better next time?

What did you do well today?

What can you look forward to tomorrow?

Did you do what was appropriate to complete your tasks?	**YES / NO**
Did you complete your knockout list?	**YES / NO**
Are you closer to your goals today?	**YES / NO**
Did you behave according to your principles?	**YES / NO**

Fill in your Gratitude Log and 28 Day Tracking

Evening Reading:

Meditate ☐
(pg 659)

WEDNESDAY — WEEK 1, DAY 4
MORNING PREPARATION

DATE:

How long did you sleep?   Meditate ☐   Morning Reading:
                                 (pg 658)
How well did you sleep?   /5   Exercise ☐

NOTES:

Review your 7-day goals. With those goals in mind, make a **'Knockout List'** of 3-5 tasks you must work to complete today. Specify the tasks, and make them something you expect you can achieve today.

What are some obstacles you are likely to face today?

What can you do to prepare for or reduce the chances of them happening?

What should you do if these obstacles happen?

> "To thine own self be true"
>
> *- Shakespeare*

(See pg 656 for writing prompts)

EVENING REVIEW

BREAKFAST	LUNCH	SUPPER	SNACKS

What were the most significant obstacles you faced today?

How could these obstacles have been worse?

How did you or how can you mitigate these obstacles?

How can you reduce the chances of them reoccurring?

How can these obstacles benefit you?

What mistakes did you make today?

What could you have done that would have been worse?

What can you do to mitigate these mistakes?

What could you do better next time?

What did you do well today?

What can you look forward to tomorrow?

Did you do what was appropriate to complete your tasks?	YES / NO
Did you complete your knockout list?	YES / NO
Are you closer to your goals today?	YES / NO
Did you behave according to your principles?	YES / NO

Fill in your Gratitude Log and 28 Day Tracking

Evening Reading:

Meditate ☐
(pg 659)

THURSDAY
MORNING PREPARATION
WEEK 1, DAY 5

DATE:

How long did you sleep? Meditate ☐ Morning Reading:
(pg 658)

How well did you sleep? /5 Exercise ☐

NOTES:

Review your 7-day goals. With those goals in mind, make a **'Knockout List'** of 3-5 tasks you must work to complete today. Specify the tasks, and make them something you expect you can achieve today.

What are some obstacles you are likely to face today?

What can you do to prepare for or reduce the chances of them happening?

What should you do if these obstacles happen?

> "To lie deliberately is to blaspheme - the liar commits deceit, and this injustice. And likewise to lie without realizing it. Because involuntary liar disrupts the harmony of nature - its order."
> — *Marcus Aurelius*

(See pg 656 for writing prompts)

EVENING REVIEW

BREAKFAST	LUNCH	SUPPER	SNACKS

What were the most significant obstacles you faced today?

How could these obstacles have been worse?

How did you or how can you mitigate these obstacles?

How can you reduce the chances of them reoccurring?

How can these obstacles benefit you?

What mistakes did you make today?

What could you have done that would have been worse?

What can you do to mitigate these mistakes?

What could you do better next time?

What did you do well today?

What can you look forward to tomorrow?

Did you do what was appropriate to complete your tasks?	**YES / NO**
Did you complete your knockout list?	**YES / NO**
Are you closer to your goals today?	**YES / NO**
Did you behave according to your principles?	**YES / NO**

Fill in your Gratitude Log and 28 Day Tracking

Evening Reading:

Meditate ☐
(pg 659)

FRIDAY
MORNING PREPARATION
WEEK 1, DAY 6

DATE:

How long did you sleep? Meditate ☐   Morning Reading:
(pg 658)

How well did you sleep? /5   Exercise ☐

NOTES:

Review your 7-day goals. With those goals in mind, make a **'Knockout List'** of 3-5 tasks you must work to complete today. Specify the tasks, and make them something you expect you can achieve today.

What are some obstacles you are likely to face today?

What can you do to prepare for or reduce the chances of them happening?

What should you do if these obstacles happen?

"If someone is able to show me that what I think or do is not right, I will happily change, for I seek the truth, by which no one was ever truly harmed. It is the person who continues in his self-deception and ignorance who is harmed."

- Marcus Aurelius

(See pg 656 for writing prompts)

EVENING REVIEW

BREAKFAST	LUNCH	SUPPER	SNACKS

What were the most significant obstacles you faced today?

How could these obstacles have been worse?

How did you or how can you mitigate these obstacles?

How can you reduce the chances of them reoccurring?

How can these obstacles benefit you?

What mistakes did you make today?

What could you have done that would have been worse?

What can you do to mitigate these mistakes?

What could you do better next time?

What did you do well today?

What can you look forward to tomorrow?

Did you do what was appropriate to complete your tasks?	**YES / NO**
Did you complete your knockout list?	**YES / NO**
Are you closer to your goals today?	**YES / NO**
Did you behave according to your principles?	**YES / NO**

Fill in your Gratitude Log and 28 Day Tracking

Evening Reading:

Meditate ☐
(pg 659)

SATURDAY   WEEK 1, DAY 7
MORNING PREPARATION

DATE:

How long did you sleep?   Meditate ☐   Morning Reading:
(pg 658)

How well did you sleep? /5   Exercise ☐

NOTES:

Review your 7-day goals. With those goals in mind, make a **'Knockout List'** of 3-5 tasks you must work to complete today. Specify the tasks, and make them something you expect you can achieve today.

What are some obstacles you are likely to face today?

What can you do to prepare for or reduce the chances of them happening?

What should you do if these obstacles happen?

> "He who follows reason in all things is both tranquil and active at the same time, and also cheerful and collected."
> *- Marcus Aurelius*

(See pg 656 for writing prompts)

EVENING REVIEW

BREAKFAST	LUNCH	SUPPER	SNACKS

What were the most significant obstacles you faced today?

How could these obstacles have been worse?

How did you or how can you mitigate these obstacles?

How can you reduce the chances of them reoccurring?

How can these obstacles benefit you?

What mistakes did you make today?

What could you have done that would have been worse?

What can you do to mitigate these mistakes?

What could you do better next time?

What did you do well today?

What can you look forward to tomorrow?

Did you do what was appropriate to complete your tasks?	**YES / NO**
Did you complete your knockout list?	**YES / NO**
Are you closer to your goals today?	**YES / NO**
Did you behave according to your principles?	**YES / NO**

Fill in your Gratitude Log and 28 Day Tracking

Evening Reading:

Meditate ☐
(pg 659)

WEEK 1 GRATITUDE LOG

Write briefly about anything that you have to be grateful for for each day.

If you are having difficulty thinking about what to write, you can consult the prompts on page 657.

SUNDAY

MONDAY

TUESDAY

WEDNESDAY

THURSDAY

FRIDAY

SATURDAY

WEEKLY PREMEDITATION OF OBSTACLES

Think of a significant obstacle happening to you, or think about suffering a significant loss. Imagine it as if it were happening now. Describe it in detail.

What would be the best way to react to this happening?

What are some things you now enjoy which you could no longer enjoy if this happens to you? Describe what you enjoy about it in detail.

How could you repair any damage caused if this happened?

What could you still enjoy in your life if this happened?

What could you do to prepare for or reduce the chances of this happening?

It's a possibility that this could happen to you. But it hasn't yet. What can you do to appreciate what you have now?

WEEK 1 REVIEW

○ Review your 7-day goals. Did you accomplish them? **YES / NO**
If no, consider why not, and if it is still worth your time. If it is, migrate it forward into a future task.

What were the best things that happened this week?

Which activities did not work well for you this week?

What activities worked well for you this week?

Overall, this week was:

7-DAY GOAL SETTING - WEEK 2

Review your 28 day goals. Consider the steps you should do to achieve the goals, and what you can do to reduce the chances of the obstacles you anticipated. With those in mind, what are your goals for the next 7 days? Make them specific and achievable in 7 days.

Why are these steps important?

What part of these steps are in your control?

WEEKLY THEME

Focus on what you can control

WEEKLY REFLECTION

(See pg 656 for writing prompts)

WEEK 2 PLANNER

	SUNDAY	MONDAY	TUESDAY

	WEDNESDAY	THURSDAY	FRIDAY	SATURDAY

SUNDAY — WEEK 2, DAY 1
MORNING PREPARATION

DATE:

How long did you sleep? Meditate ☐   Morning Reading:
(pg 658)

How well did you sleep? /5 Exercise ☐

NOTES:

Review your 7-day goals. With those goals in mind, make a **'Knockout List'** of 3-5 tasks you must work to complete today. Specify the tasks, and make them something you expect you can achieve today.

What are some obstacles you are likely to face today?

What can you do to prepare for or reduce the chances of them happening?

What should you do if these obstacles happen?

> "The chief task in life is simply this: to identify and separate matters so that I can say clearly to myself which are externals not under my control, and which have to do with the choices I actually control."
>
> *- Epictetus*

(See pg 656 for writing prompts)

EVENTING REVIEW

BREAKFAST	LUNCH	SUPPER	SNACKS

What were the most significant obstacles you faced today?

How could these obstacles have been worse?

How did you or how can you mitigate these obstacles?

How can you reduce the chances of them reoccurring?

How can these obstacles benefit you?

What mistakes did you make today?

What could you have done that would have been worse?

What can you do to mitigate these mistakes?

What could you do better next time?

What did you do well today?

What can you look forward to tomorrow?

Did you do what was appropriate to complete your tasks?	**YES / NO**
Did you complete your knockout list?	**YES / NO**
Are you closer to your goals today?	**YES / NO**
Did you behave according to your principles?	**YES / NO**

◯ Fill in your Gratitude Log and 28 Day Tracking

Evening Reading:

Meditate ☐
(pg 659)

MONDAY — MORNING PREPARATION
WEEK 2, DAY 2

DATE:

How long did you sleep?   Meditate ☐   Morning Reading:
(pg 658)

How well did you sleep? /5   Exercise ☐

NOTES:

Review your 7-day goals. With those goals in mind, make a **'Knockout List'** of 3-5 tasks you must work to complete today. Specify the tasks, and make them something you expect you can achieve today.

What are some obstacles you are likely to face today?

What can you do to prepare for or reduce the chances of them happening?

What should you do if these obstacles happen?

> "Just that you do the right thing. The rest doesn't matter. Cold or warm. Tired or well-rested. Despised or honored. Dying...or busy with other assignments."
> — *Marcus Aurelius*

(See pg 656 for writing prompts)

EVENING REVIEW

BREAKFAST	LUNCH	SUPPER	SNACKS

What were the most significant obstacles you faced today?

How could these obstacles have been worse?

How did you or how can you mitigate these obstacles?

How can you reduce the chances of them reoccurring?

How can these obstacles benefit you?

What mistakes did you make today?

What could you have done that would have been worse?

What can you do to mitigate these mistakes?

What could you do better next time?

What did you do well today?

What can you look forward to tomorrow?

Did you do what was appropriate to complete your tasks?	**YES / NO**
Did you complete your knockout list?	**YES / NO**
Are you closer to your goals today?	**YES / NO**
Did you behave according to your principles?	**YES / NO**

Fill in your Gratitude Log and 28 Day Tracking

Evening Reading:

Meditate ☐
(pg 659)

TUESDAY — MORNING PREPARATION
WEEK 2, DAY 3

DATE:

How long did you sleep?   Meditate ☐   Morning Reading:
(pg 658)
How well did you sleep? /5   Exercise ☐

NOTES:

Review your 7-day goals. With those goals in mind, make a **'Knockout List'** of 3-5 tasks you must work to complete today. Specify the tasks, and make them something you expect you can achieve today.

What are some obstacles you are likely to face today?

What can you do to prepare for or reduce the chances of them happening?

What should you do if these obstacles happen?

> "He is most powerful who has power over himself"
> — *Seneca*

(See pg 656 for writing prompts)

EVENING REVIEW

BREAKFAST	LUNCH	SUPPER	SNACKS

What were the most significant obstacles you faced today?

How could these obstacles have been worse?

How did you or how can you mitigate these obstacles?

How can you reduce the chances of them reoccurring?

How can these obstacles benefit you?

What mistakes did you make today?

What could you have done that would have been worse?

What can you do to mitigate these mistakes?

What could you do better next time?

What did you do well today?

What can you look forward to tomorrow?

Did you do what was appropriate to complete your tasks?	**YES / NO**
Did you complete your knockout list?	**YES / NO**
Are you closer to your goals today?	**YES / NO**
Did you behave according to your principles?	**YES / NO**

◯ Fill in your Gratitude Log and 28 Day Tracking

Evening Reading:

Meditate ☐
(pg 659)

WEDNESDAY — WEEK 2, DAY 4
MORNING PREPARATION

DATE:

How long did you sleep?   Meditate ☐   Morning Reading:
(pg 658)

How well did you sleep? /5   Exercise ☐

NOTES:

Review your 7-day goals. With those goals in mind, make a **'Knockout List'** of 3-5 tasks you must work to complete today. Specify the tasks, and make them something you expect you can achieve today.

What are some obstacles you are likely to face today?

What can you do to prepare for or reduce the chances of them happening?

What should you do if these obstacles happen?

> "Gratitude is not only greatest of the virtues, but parent of all others."
> *- Cicero*

(See pg 656 for writing prompts)

EVENING REVIEW

BREAKFAST	LUNCH	SUPPER	SNACKS

What were the most significant obstacles you faced today?

How could these obstacles have been worse?

How did you or how can you mitigate these obstacles?

How can you reduce the chances of them reoccurring?

How can these obstacles benefit you?

What mistakes did you make today?

What could you have done that would have been worse?

What can you do to mitigate these mistakes?

What could you do better next time?

What did you do well today?

What can you look forward to tomorrow?

Did you do what was appropriate to complete your tasks?	**YES / NO**
Did you complete your knockout list?	**YES / NO**
Are you closer to your goals today?	**YES / NO**
Did you behave according to your principles?	**YES / NO**

○ Fill in your Gratitude Log and 28 Day Tracking

Evening Reading:

Meditate ☐
(pg 659)

THURSDAY — WEEK 2, DAY 5
MORNING PREPARATION

DATE:

How long did you sleep? Meditate ☐ (pg 658)

How well did you sleep? /5 Exercise ☐

Morning Reading:

NOTES:

Review your 7-day goals. With those goals in mind, make a **'Knockout List'** of 3-5 tasks you must work to complete today. Specify the tasks, and make them something you expect you can achieve today.

What are some obstacles you are likely to face today?

What can you do to prepare for or reduce the chances of them happening?

What should you do if these obstacles happen?

"The soul is dyed the color of its thoughts. Think only on those things that are in line with your principles and can bear the light of day. The content of your character is your choice. Day by day, what you do is who you become. Your integrity is your destiny - it is the light that guides your way."

- Heraclitus

(See pg 656 for writing prompts)

EVENTING REVIEW

BREAKFAST	LUNCH	SUPPER	SNACKS

What were the most significant obstacles you faced today?

How could these obstacles have been worse?

How did you or how can you mitigate these obstacles?

How can you reduce the chances of them reoccurring?

How can these obstacles benefit you?

What mistakes did you make today?

What could you have done that would have been worse?

What can you do to mitigate these mistakes?

What could you do better next time?

What did you do well today?

What can you look forward to tomorrow?

Did you do what was appropriate to complete your tasks?	**YES / NO**
Did you complete your knockout list?	**YES / NO**
Are you closer to your goals today?	**YES / NO**
Did you behave according to your principles?	**YES / NO**

◯ Fill in your Gratitude Log and 28 Day Tracking

Evening Reading:

Meditate ☐
(pg 659)

FRIDAY
MORNING PREPARATION
WEEK 2, DAY 6

DATE:

How long did you sleep? Meditate ☐ | Morning Reading:
(pg 658)

How well did you sleep? /5 Exercise ☐

NOTES:

Review your 7-day goals. With those goals in mind, make a **'Knockout List'** of 3-5 tasks you must work to complete today. Specify the tasks, and make them something you expect you can achieve today.

What are some obstacles you are likely to face today?

What can you do to prepare for or reduce the chances of them happening?

What should you do if these obstacles happen?

> "He is richest who is content with the least, for content is the wealth of nature."
> — *Socrates*

(See pg 656 for writing prompts)

EVENING REVIEW

BREAKFAST	LUNCH	SUPPER	SNACKS

What were the most significant obstacles you faced today?

How could these obstacles have been worse?

How did you or how can you mitigate these obstacles?

How can you reduce the chances of them reoccurring?

How can these obstacles benefit you?

What mistakes did you make today?

What could you have done that would have been worse?

What can you do to mitigate these mistakes?

What could you do better next time?

What did you do well today?

What can you look forward to tomorrow?

Did you do what was appropriate to complete your tasks?	**YES / NO**
Did you complete your knockout list?	**YES / NO**
Are you closer to your goals today?	**YES / NO**
Did you behave according to your principles?	**YES / NO**

Fill in your Gratitude Log and 28 Day Tracking

Evening Reading:

Meditate ☐
(pg 659)

SATURDAY
MORNING PREPARATION
WEEK 2, DAY 7

DATE:

How long did you sleep?   Meditate ☐   Morning Reading:
(pg 658)

How well did you sleep? /5   Exercise ☐

NOTES:

Review your 7-day goals. With those goals in mind, make a **'Knockout List'** of 3-5 tasks you must work to complete today. Specify the tasks, and make them something you expect you can achieve today.

What are some obstacles you are likely to face today?

What can you do to prepare for or reduce the chances of them happening?

What should you do if these obstacles happen?

> "If you are ever tempted to look for outside approval, realize that you have compromised your integrity."
> *-Epictetus*

(See pg 656 for writing prompts)

EVENTING REVIEW

BREAKFAST	LUNCH	SUPPER	SNACKS

What were the most significant obstacles you faced today?

How could these obstacles have been worse?

How did you or how can you mitigate these obstacles?

How can you reduce the chances of them reoccurring?

How can these obstacles benefit you?

What mistakes did you make today?

What could you have done that would have been worse?

What can you do to mitigate these mistakes?

What could you do better next time?

What did you do well today?

What can you look forward to tomorrow?

Did you do what was appropriate to complete your tasks?	**YES / NO**
Did you complete your knockout list?	**YES / NO**
Are you closer to your goals today?	**YES / NO**
Did you behave according to your principles?	**YES / NO**

Fill in your Gratitude Log and 28 Day Tracking

Evening Reading:

Meditate ☐
(pg 659)

WEEK 2 GRATITUDE LOG

Write briefly about anything that you have to be grateful for for each day.

If you are having difficulty thinking about what to write, you can consult the prompts on page 657.

SUNDAY

MONDAY

TUESDAY

WEDNESDAY

THURSDAY

FRIDAY

SATURDAY

WEEKLY PREMEDITATION OF OBSTACLES

Think of a significant obstacle happening to you, or think about suffering a significant loss. Imagine it as if it were happening now. Describe it in detail.

What would be the best way to react to this happening?

What are some things you now enjoy which you could no longer enjoy if this happens to you? Describe what you enjoy about it in detail.

How could you repair any damage caused if this happened?

What could you still enjoy in your life if this happened?

What could you do to prepare for or reduce the chances of this happening?

It's a possibility that this could happen to you. But it hasn't yet. What can you do to appreciate what you have now?

WEEK 2 REVIEW

○ Review your 7-day goals. Did you accomplish them? **YES / NO**
If no, consider why not, and if it is still worth your time. If it is, migrate it forward into a future task.

What were the best things that happened this week?

Which activities did not work well for you this week?

What activities worked well for you this week?

Overall, this week was:

7-DAY GOAL SETTING - WEEK 3

Review your 28 day goals. Consider the steps you should do to achieve the goals, and what you can do to reduce the chances of the obstacles you anticipated. With those in mind, what are your goals for the next 7 days? Make them specific and achievable in 7 days.

Why are these steps important?

What part of these steps are in your control?

WEEKLY THEME

Seek Excellence

WEEKLY REFLECTION

(See pg 656 for writing prompts)

WEEK 3 PLANNER

	SUNDAY	MONDAY	TUESDAY

	WEDNESDAY	THURSDAY	FRIDAY	SATURDAY

SUNDAY — WEEK 3, DAY 1
MORNING PREPARATION

DATE:

How long did you sleep?   Meditate ☐
(pg 658)

How well did you sleep? /5   Exercise ☐

Morning Reading:

NOTES:

Review your 7-day goals. With those goals in mind, make a **'Knockout List'** of 3-5 tasks you must work to complete today. Specify the tasks, and make them something you expect you can achieve today.

What are some obstacles you are likely to face today?

What can you do to prepare for or reduce the chances of them happening?

What should you do if these obstacles happen?

> ## 'The unexamined life is not worth living'
>
> ### *- Socrates*

(See pg 656 for writing prompts)

EVENING REVIEW

BREAKFAST	LUNCH	SUPPER	SNACKS

What were the most significant obstacles you faced today?

How could these obstacles have been worse?

How did you or how can you mitigate these obstacles?

How can you reduce the chances of them reoccurring?

How can these obstacles benefit you?

What mistakes did you make today?

What could you have done that would have been worse?

What can you do to mitigate these mistakes?

What could you do better next time?

What did you do well today?

What can you look forward to tomorrow?

Did you do what was appropriate to complete your tasks?	YES / NO
Did you complete your knockout list?	YES / NO
Are you closer to your goals today?	YES / NO
Did you behave according to your principles?	YES / NO

Fill in your Gratitude Log and 28 Day Tracking

Evening Reading:

Meditate ☐
(pg 659)

MONDAY — WEEK 3, DAY 2
MORNING PREPARATION

DATE:

How long did you sleep?   Meditate ☐ (pg 658)

How well did you sleep? /5   Exercise ☐

Morning Reading:

NOTES:

Review your 7-day goals. With those goals in mind, make a **'Knockout List'** of 3-5 tasks you must work to complete today. Specify the tasks, and make them something you expect you can achieve today.

What are some obstacles you are likely to face today?

What can you do to prepare for or reduce the chances of them happening?

What should you do if these obstacles happen?

> "Progress is not achieved by luck or accident, but by working on yourself daily."
>
> *- Epictetus*

(See pg 656 for writing prompts)

EVENING REVIEW

BREAKFAST	LUNCH	SUPPER	SNACKS

What were the most significant obstacles you faced today?

How could these obstacles have been worse?

How did you or how can you mitigate these obstacles?

How can you reduce the chances of them reoccurring?

How can these obstacles benefit you?

What mistakes did you make today?

What could you have done that would have been worse?

What can you do to mitigate these mistakes?

What could you do better next time?

What did you do well today?

What can you look forward to tomorrow?

Did you do what was appropriate to complete your tasks?	**YES / NO**
Did you complete your knockout list?	**YES / NO**
Are you closer to your goals today?	**YES / NO**
Did you behave according to your principles?	**YES / NO**

Fill in your Gratitude Log and 28 Day Tracking

Evening Reading:

Meditate ☐
(pg 659)

TUESDAY — MORNING PREPARATION
WEEK 3, DAY 3

DATE:

How long did you sleep? Meditate ☐   Morning Reading:
(pg 658)

How well did you sleep? /5   Exercise ☐

NOTES:

Review your 7-day goals. With those goals in mind, make a **'Knockout List'** of 3-5 tasks you must work to complete today. Specify the tasks, and make them something you expect you can achieve today.

What are some obstacles you are likely to face today?

What can you do to prepare for or reduce the chances of them happening?

What should you do if these obstacles happen?

> One should seek virtue for its own sake and not from hope or fear, or any external motive. It is in virtue that happiness consists, for virtue is the state of mind which tends to make the whole of life harmonious.
>
> *- Zeno of Citium*

(See pg 656 for writing prompts)

EVENTING REVIEW

BREAKFAST	LUNCH	SUPPER	SNACKS

What were the most significant obstacles you faced today?

How could these obstacles have been worse?

How did you or how can you mitigate these obstacles?

How can you reduce the chances of them reoccurring?

How can these obstacles benefit you?

What mistakes did you make today?

What could you have done that would have been worse?

What can you do to mitigate these mistakes?

What could you do better next time?

What did you do well today?

What can you look forward to tomorrow?

Did you do what was appropriate to complete your tasks?	**YES / NO**
Did you complete your knockout list?	**YES / NO**
Are you closer to your goals today?	**YES / NO**
Did you behave according to your principles?	**YES / NO**

Fill in your Gratitude Log and 28 Day Tracking

Evening Reading:

Meditate ☐
(pg 659)

WEDNESDAY
MORNING PREPARATION
WEEK 3, DAY 4

DATE:

How long did you sleep?   Meditate ☐   Morning Reading:
(pg 658)

How well did you sleep? /5   Exercise ☐

NOTES:

Review your 7-day goals. With those goals in mind, make a **'Knockout List'** of 3-5 tasks you must work to complete today. Specify the tasks, and make them something you expect you can achieve today.

What are some obstacles you are likely to face today?

What can you do to prepare for or reduce the chances of them happening?

What should you do if these obstacles happen?

"Because a thing seems difficult for you, do not think it impossible for anyone to accomplish."
- *Marcus Aurelius*

(See pg 656 for writing prompts)

EVENING REVIEW

BREAKFAST	LUNCH	SUPPER	SNACKS

What were the most significant obstacles you faced today?

How could these obstacles have been worse?

How did you or how can you mitigate these obstacles?

How can you reduce the chances of them reoccurring?

How can these obstacles benefit you?

What mistakes did you make today?

What could you have done that would have been worse?

What can you do to mitigate these mistakes?

What could you do better next time?

What did you do well today?

What can you look forward to tomorrow?

Did you do what was appropriate to complete your tasks?	**YES / NO**
Did you complete your knockout list?	**YES / NO**
Are you closer to your goals today?	**YES / NO**
Did you behave according to your principles?	**YES / NO**

◯ Fill in your Gratitude Log and 28 Day Tracking

Evening Reading:

Meditate ☐
(pg 659)

THURSDAY
MORNING PREPARATION
WEEK 3, DAY 5

DATE:

How long did you sleep?   Meditate ☐   Morning Reading:
(pg 658)

How well did you sleep? /5   Exercise ☐

NOTES:

Review your 7-day goals. With those goals in mind, make a **'Knockout List'** of 3-5 tasks you must work to complete today. Specify the tasks, and make them something you expect you can achieve today.

What are some obstacles you are likely to face today?

What can you do to prepare for or reduce the chances of them happening?

What should you do if these obstacles happen?

> "Become acquainted with every art.
> Know the Ways of all professions."
>
> *- Miyamoto Musashi*

(See pg 656 for writing prompts)

EVENING REVIEW

BREAKFAST	LUNCH	SUPPER	SNACKS

What were the most significant obstacles you faced today?

How could these obstacles have been worse?

How did you or how can you mitigate these obstacles?

How can you reduce the chances of them reoccurring?

How can these obstacles benefit you?

What mistakes did you make today?

What could you have done that would have been worse?

What can you do to mitigate these mistakes?

What could you do better next time?

What did you do well today?

What can you look forward to tomorrow?

Did you do what was appropriate to complete your tasks?	**YES / NO**
Did you complete your knockout list?	**YES / NO**
Are you closer to your goals today?	**YES / NO**
Did you behave according to your principles?	**YES / NO**

Fill in your Gratitude Log and 28 Day Tracking

Evening Reading:

Meditate ☐
(pg 659)

FRIDAY   WEEK 3, DAY 6
MORNING PREPARATION

DATE:

How long did you sleep?   Meditate ☐   Morning Reading:
(pg 658)

How well did you sleep?   /5   Exercise ☐

NOTES:

Review your 7-day goals. With those goals in mind, make a **'Knockout List'** of 3-5 tasks you must work to complete today. Specify the tasks, and make them something you expect you can achieve today.

What are some obstacles you are likely to face today?

What can you do to prepare for or reduce the chances of them happening?

What should you do if these obstacles happen?

"Take the case of one whose task it is to shoot a spear or arrow straight at some target. One's ultimate aim is to do all in one's power to shoot straight, and the same applies with our ultimate goal. In this kind of example, it is to shoot straight that one must do all one can; none the less, it is to do all one can to accomplish the task that is really the ultimate aim. It is just the same with what we call the supreme good in life. To actually hit the target is, as we say, to be selected but not sought."

- Cicero

(See pg 656 for writing prompts)

EVENTING REVIEW

BREAKFAST	LUNCH	SUPPER	SNACKS

What were the most significant obstacles you faced today?

How could these obstacles have been worse?

How did you or how can you mitigate these obstacles?

How can you reduce the chances of them reoccurring?

How can these obstacles benefit you?

What mistakes did you make today?

What could you have done that would have been worse?

What can you do to mitigate these mistakes?

What could you do better next time?

What did you do well today?

What can you look forward to tomorrow?

Did you do what was appropriate to complete your tasks?	**YES / NO**
Did you complete your knockout list?	**YES / NO**
Are you closer to your goals today?	**YES / NO**
Did you behave according to your principles?	**YES / NO**

Fill in your Gratitude Log and 28 Day Tracking

Evening Reading:

Meditate ☐
(pg 659)

SATURDAY — MORNING PREPARATION
WEEK 3, DAY 7

DATE:

How long did you sleep?   Meditate ☐   Morning Reading:
(pg 658)

How well did you sleep? /5   Exercise ☐

NOTES:

Review your 7-day goals. With those goals in mind, make a **'Knockout List'** of 3-5 tasks you must work to complete today. Specify the tasks, and make them something you expect you can achieve today.

What are some obstacles you are likely to face today?

What can you do to prepare for or reduce the chances of them happening?

What should you do if these obstacles happen?

One should spend their whole lifetime diligently learning as much as they can. In this way you will become a more developed and fully realised human being with each passing day. The goal of total perfection has no end.

(See pg 656 for writing prompts)

EVENING REVIEW

BREAKFAST	LUNCH	SUPPER	SNACKS

What were the most significant obstacles you faced today?

How could these obstacles have been worse?

How did you or how can you mitigate these obstacles?

How can you reduce the chances of them reoccurring?

How can these obstacles benefit you?

What mistakes did you make today?

What could you have done that would have been worse?

What can you do to mitigate these mistakes?

What could you do better next time?

What did you do well today?

What can you look forward to tomorrow?

Did you do what was appropriate to complete your tasks?	**YES / NO**
Did you complete your knockout list?	**YES / NO**
Are you closer to your goals today?	**YES / NO**
Did you behave according to your principles?	**YES / NO**

Fill in your Gratitude Log and 28 Day Tracking

Evening Reading:

Meditate ☐
(pg 659)

WEEK 3 GRATITUDE LOG

Write briefly about anything that you have to be grateful for for each day.

If you are having difficulty thinking about what to write, you can consult the prompts on page 657.

SUNDAY

MONDAY

TUESDAY

WEDNESDAY

THURSDAY

FRIDAY

SATURDAY

WEEKLY PREMEDITATION OF OBSTACLES

Think of a significant obstacle happening to you, or think about suffering a significant loss. Imagine it as if it were happening now. Describe it in detail.

What would be the best way to react to this happening?

What are some things you now enjoy which you could no longer enjoy if this happens to you? Describe what you enjoy about it in detail.

How could you repair any damage caused if this happened?

What could you still enjoy in your life if this happened?

What could you do to prepare for or reduce the chances of this happening?

It's a possibility that this could happen to you. But it hasn't yet. What can you do to appreciate what you have now?

WEEK 3 REVIEW

○ Review your 7-day goals. Did you accomplish them? **YES / NO**
If no, consider why not, and if it is still worth your time. If it is, migrate it forward into a future task.

What were the best things that happened this week?

Which activities did not work well for you this week?

What activities worked well for you this week?

Overall, this week was:

7-DAY GOAL SETTING - WEEK 4

Review your 28 day goals. Consider the steps you should do to achieve the goals, and what you can do to reduce the chances of the obstacles you anticipated. With those in mind, what are your goals for the next 7 days? Make them specific and achievable in 7 days.

Why are these steps important?

What part of these steps are in your control?

WEEKLY THEME

Be Present

WEEKLY REFLECTION

(See pg 656 for writing prompts)

WEEK 4 PLANNER

	SUNDAY	MONDAY	TUESDAY

	WEDNESDAY	THURSDAY	FRIDAY	SATURDAY

SUNDAY — WEEK 4, DAY 1
MORNING PREPARATION

DATE:

How long did you sleep? Meditate ☐   Morning Reading:
(pg 658)

How well did you sleep? /5   Exercise ☐

NOTES:

Review your 7-day goals. With those goals in mind, make a **'Knockout List'** of 3-5 tasks you must work to complete today. Specify the tasks, and make them something you expect you can achieve today.

What are some obstacles you are likely to face today?

What can you do to prepare for or reduce the chances of them happening?

What should you do if these obstacles happen?

> "Dwell on the beauty of life. Watch the stars, and see yourself running with them."
>
> — *Marcus Aurelius*

(See pg 656 for writing prompts)

EVENING REVIEW

BREAKFAST	LUNCH	SUPPER	SNACKS

What were the most significant obstacles you faced today?

How could these obstacles have been worse?

How did you or how can you mitigate these obstacles?

How can you reduce the chances of them reoccurring?

How can these obstacles benefit you?

What mistakes did you make today?

What could you have done that would have been worse?

What can you do to mitigate these mistakes?

What could you do better next time?

What did you do well today?

What can you look forward to tomorrow?

Did you do what was appropriate to complete your tasks?	**YES / NO**
Did you complete your knockout list?	**YES / NO**
Are you closer to your goals today?	**YES / NO**
Did you behave according to your principles?	**YES / NO**

Fill in your Gratitude Log and 28 Day Tracking

Evening Reading:

Meditate ☐
(pg 659)

MONDAY — WEEK 4, DAY 2
MORNING PREPARATION

DATE:

How long did you sleep? Meditate ☐ Morning Reading:
(pg 658)

How well did you sleep? /5   Exercise ☐

NOTES:

Review your 7-day goals. With those goals in mind, make a **'Knockout List'** of 3-5 tasks you must work to complete today. Specify the tasks, and make them something you expect you can achieve today.

What are some obstacles you are likely to face today?

What can you do to prepare for or reduce the chances of them happening?

What should you do if these obstacles happen?

> "I will keep constant watch over myself and — most usefully — will put each day up for review. For this is what makes us evil — that none of us looks back upon our own lives. We reflect upon only that which we are about to do. And yet our plans for the future descend from the past."
>
> *- Seneca*

(See pg 656 for writing prompts)

EVENING REVIEW

BREAKFAST	LUNCH	SUPPER	SNACKS

What were the most significant obstacles you faced today?

How could these obstacles have been worse?

How did you or how can you mitigate these obstacles?

How can you reduce the chances of them reoccurring?

How can these obstacles benefit you?

What mistakes did you make today?

What could you have done that would have been worse?

What can you do to mitigate these mistakes?

What could you do better next time?

What did you do well today?

What can you look forward to tomorrow?

Did you do what was appropriate to complete your tasks?	**YES / NO**
Did you complete your knockout list?	**YES / NO**
Are you closer to your goals today?	**YES / NO**
Did you behave according to your principles?	**YES / NO**

Fill in your Gratitude Log and 28 Day Tracking

Evening Reading:

Meditate ☐
(pg 659)

TUESDAY
MORNING PREPARATION
WEEK 4, DAY 3

DATE:

How long did you sleep? Meditate ☐   Morning Reading:
(pg 658)

How well did you sleep? /5   Exercise ☐

NOTES:

Review your 7-day goals. With those goals in mind, make a **'Knockout List'** of 3-5 tasks you must work to complete today. Specify the tasks, and make them something you expect you can achieve today.

What are some obstacles you are likely to face today?

What can you do to prepare for or reduce the chances of them happening?

What should you do if these obstacles happen?

"Two elements must therefore be rooted out once for all, - the fear of future suffering, and the recollection of past suffering; since the latter no longer concerns me, and the former concerns me not yet."

— *Seneca*

(See pg 656 for writing prompts)

EVENING REVIEW

BREAKFAST	LUNCH	SUPPER	SNACKS

What were the most significant obstacles you faced today?

How could these obstacles have been worse?

How did you or how can you mitigate these obstacles?

How can you reduce the chances of them reoccurring?

How can these obstacles benefit you?

What mistakes did you make today?

What could you have done that would have been worse?

What can you do to mitigate these mistakes?

What could you do better next time?

What did you do well today?

What can you look forward to tomorrow?

Did you do what was appropriate to complete your tasks?	**YES / NO**
Did you complete your knockout list?	**YES / NO**
Are you closer to your goals today?	**YES / NO**
Did you behave according to your principles?	**YES / NO**

Fill in your Gratitude Log and 28 Day Tracking

Evening Reading:

Meditate ☐
(pg 659)

WEDNESDAY — WEEK 4, DAY 4
MORNING PREPARATION

DATE:

How long did you sleep?   Meditate ☐   Morning Reading:
                            (pg 658)
How well did you sleep? /5 Exercise ☐

NOTES:

Review your 7-day goals. With those goals in mind, make a **'Knockout List'** of 3-5 tasks you must work to complete today. Specify the tasks, and make them something you expect you can achieve today.

What are some obstacles you are likely to face today?

What can you do to prepare for or reduce the chances of them happening?

What should you do if these obstacles happen?

> "Concentrate every minute like a Roman - like a man - on doing what's in front of you with precise and genuine seriousness, tenderly, willingly, with justice."
> - *Marcus Aurelius*

(See pg 656 for writing prompts)

EVENING REVIEW

BREAKFAST	LUNCH	SUPPER	SNACKS

What were the most significant obstacles you faced today?

How could these obstacles have been worse?

How did you or how can you mitigate these obstacles?

How can you reduce the chances of them reoccurring?

How can these obstacles benefit you?

What mistakes did you make today?

What could you have done that would have been worse?

What can you do to mitigate these mistakes?

What could you do better next time?

What did you do well today?

What can you look forward to tomorrow?

Did you do what was appropriate to complete your tasks?	**YES / NO**
Did you complete your knockout list?	**YES / NO**
Are you closer to your goals today?	**YES / NO**
Did you behave according to your principles?	**YES / NO**

Fill in your Gratitude Log and 28 Day Tracking

Evening Reading:

Meditate ☐
(pg 659)

THURSDAY
MORNING PREPARATION
WEEK 4, DAY 5

DATE:

How long did you sleep?   Meditate ☐   Morning Reading:
(pg 658)

How well did you sleep? /5   Exercise ☐

NOTES:

Review your 7-day goals. With those goals in mind, make a **'Knockout List'** of 3-5 tasks you must work to complete today. Specify the tasks, and make them something you expect you can achieve today.

What are some obstacles you are likely to face today?

What can you do to prepare for or reduce the chances of them happening?

What should you do if these obstacles happen?

> "No person has the power to have everything they want, but it is in their power not to want what they don't have, and to cheerfully put to good use what they do have."
>
> - *Seneca*

(See pg 656 for writing prompts)

EVENING REVIEW

BREAKFAST	LUNCH	SUPPER	SNACKS

What were the most significant obstacles you faced today?

How could these obstacles have been worse?

How did you or how can you mitigate these obstacles?

How can you reduce the chances of them reoccurring?

How can these obstacles benefit you?

What mistakes did you make today?

What could you have done that would have been worse?

What can you do to mitigate these mistakes?

What could you do better next time?

What did you do well today?

What can you look forward to tomorrow?

Did you do what was appropriate to complete your tasks?	YES / NO
Did you complete your knockout list?	YES / NO
Are you closer to your goals today?	YES / NO
Did you behave according to your principles?	YES / NO

Fill in your Gratitude Log and 28 Day Tracking

Evening Reading:

Meditate ☐
(pg 659)

FRIDAY
MORNING PREPARATION
WEEK 4, DAY 6

DATE:

How long did you sleep?   Meditate ☐   Morning Reading:
(pg 658)

How well did you sleep? /5   Exercise ☐

NOTES:

Review your 7-day goals. With those goals in mind, make a **'Knockout List'** of 3-5 tasks you must work to complete today. Specify the tasks, and make them something you expect you can achieve today.

What are some obstacles you are likely to face today?

What can you do to prepare for or reduce the chances of them happening?

What should you do if these obstacles happen?

> "Nowhere can you find a quieter or more untroubled retreat than in your own soul."
>
> *- Marcus Aurelius*

(See pg 656 for writing prompts)

EVENING REVIEW

BREAKFAST	LUNCH	SUPPER	SNACKS

What were the most significant obstacles you faced today?

How could these obstacles have been worse?

How did you or how can you mitigate these obstacles?

How can you reduce the chances of them reoccurring?

How can these obstacles benefit you?

What mistakes did you make today?

What could you have done that would have been worse?

What can you do to mitigate these mistakes?

What could you do better next time?

What did you do well today?

What can you look forward to tomorrow?

Did you do what was appropriate to complete your tasks?	**YES / NO**
Did you complete your knockout list?	**YES / NO**
Are you closer to your goals today?	**YES / NO**
Did you behave according to your principles?	**YES / NO**

○ Fill in your Gratitude Log and 28 Day Tracking

Evening Reading:

Meditate ☐
(pg 659)

SATURDAY — MORNING PREPARATION
WEEK 4, DAY 7

DATE:

How long did you sleep? Meditate ☐ Morning Reading:
(pg 658)

How well did you sleep? /5 Exercise ☐

NOTES:

Review your 7-day goals. With those goals in mind, make a **'Knockout List'** of 3-5 tasks you must work to complete today. Specify the tasks, and make them something you expect you can achieve today.

What are some obstacles you are likely to face today?

What can you do to prepare for or reduce the chances of them happening?

What should you do if these obstacles happen?

> "True happiness is to enjoy the present, without anxious dependence upon the future, not to amuse ourselves with either hopes or fears but to rest satisfied with what we have, which is sufficient, for he that is so wants nothing"
>
> — *Seneca*

(See pg 656 for writing prompts)

EVENING REVIEW

BREAKFAST	LUNCH	SUPPER	SNACKS

What were the most significant obstacles you faced today?

How could these obstacles have been worse?

How did you or how can you mitigate these obstacles?

How can you reduce the chances of them reoccurring?

How can these obstacles benefit you?

What mistakes did you make today?

What could you have done that would have been worse?

What can you do to mitigate these mistakes?

What could you do better next time?

What did you do well today?

What can you look forward to tomorrow?

Did you do what was appropriate to complete your tasks?	**YES / NO**
Did you complete your knockout list?	**YES / NO**
Are you closer to your goals today?	**YES / NO**
Did you behave according to your principles?	**YES / NO**

Fill in your Gratitude Log and 28 Day Tracking

Evening Reading:

Meditate ☐
(pg 659)

227

WEEK 4 GRATITUDE LOG

Write briefly about anything that you have to be grateful for for each day.

If you are having difficulty thinking about what to write, you can consult the prompts on page 657.

SUNDAY

MONDAY

TUESDAY

WEDNESDAY

THURSDAY

FRIDAY

SATURDAY

WEEKLY PREMEDITATION OF OBSTACLES

Think of a significant obstacle happening to you, or think about suffering a significant loss. Imagine it as if it were happening now. Describe it in detail.

What would be the best way to react to this happening?

What are some things you now enjoy which you could no longer enjoy if this happens to you? Describe what you enjoy about it in detail.

How could you repair any damage caused if this happened?

What could you still enjoy in your life if this happened?

What could you do to prepare for or reduce the chances of this happening?

It's a possibility that this could happen to you. But it hasn't yet. What can you do to appreciate what you have now?

28 DAY TRACKING - WEEKS 1-4

Week 1   Week 2

Week 3	Week 4

HEALTH & WELLNESS REVIEW - WEEKS 1-4

	CURRENT	CHANGE	TARGET
Weight			
Body Fat %			
Neck			
Shoulders			
Chest			
Right Bicep			
Left Bicep			
Right Forearm			
Left Forearm			
Waist			
Hips			
Right Thigh			
Left Thigh			
Right Calf			
Left Calf			
Push-ups in 60 seconds			
Pull-ups in 60 seconds/Flex Arm Hang			
Squats in 60 seconds			
Sit-ups in 60 seconds			
Sit & Reach Distance			
Heartbeat after 3 Min Stair Climb			

On average for the last 4 weeks, how much do you agree?
On a scale of 1-10 with 1 being least agreement and 10 being most agreement

		CURRENT	CHANGE
PHYSICAL HEALTH	I am clean and orderly		
	I am sleeping well		
	I am exercising well		
	I feel properly energetic		
	Total Physical Health Score:		
EMOTIONAL HEALTH	I am not feeling worried or anxious		
	I am able to relax		
	I feel a sense of tranquility		
	I am not easily annoyed or irritated		
	Total Emotional Health Score:		
INTELLECTUAL HEALTH	I am consistently learning		
	I can consider ideas that I disagree with		
	I can change my opinion when appropriate		
	I am intellectually challenged		
	Total Intellectual Health Score:		
SPIRITUAL HEALTH	I can forgive myself and others		
	I feel a strong purpose in my life		
	I accept what I cannot change		
	I practice routines to develop my spirit		
	Total Spiritual Health Score:		
SOCIAL HEALTH	I don't feel lonely		
	I enjoy spending time with others		
	I make a positive contribution to my community		
	I do not attempt to avoid people		
	Total Social Health Score:		

Total Score:		Change:	

WEEK 4 REVIEW

◯ Review your 7-day goals. Did you accomplish them? **YES / NO**
If no, consider why not, and if it is still worth your time. If it is, migrate it forward into a future task.

What were the best things that happened this week?

Which activities did not work well for you this week?

What activities worked well for you this week?

Overall, this week was:

28 DAY REVIEW - WEEKS 1-4

○ Review your 28-day goals. Did you accomplish them? **YES / NO**
If no, consider why not, and if it is still worth your time. If it is, migrate it forward into a future task.

What were the best things that happened these last four weeks?

Which activities did not work well for you these last four weeks?

What activities worked well for you these last four weeks?

28-DAY GOAL SETTING - WEEKS 5-8

Review pages 42 & 43. Consider the steps you should do to achieve your quarterly goals, and what you can do to reduce the chances of the obstacles you anticipated. With those in mind, what are your goals for the next 28 days? Make them specific and achievable in 28 days.

What are some obstacles you are likely to face with these goals?

What should you do if these obstacles happen?

What can you do to prepare for or reduce the chances of them happening?

7-DAY GOAL SETTING - WEEK 5

Breakdown your 28 day goals. Consider the steps you should do to achieve the goals, and what you can do to reduce the chances of the obstacles you anticipated. With those in mind, what are your goals for the next 7 days? Make them specific and achievable in 7 days.

Why are these steps important?

What part of these steps are in your control?

240

WEEKLY THEME

Take Action

WEEKLY REFLECTION

(See pg 656 for writing prompts)

245

28 DAY CALENDAR - WEEKS 5-8

	SUNDAY	MONDAY	TUESDAY
WEEK 5			
WEEK 6			
WEEK 7			
WEEK 8			

WEDNESDAY	THURSDAY	FRIDAY	SATURDAY

WEEK 5 PLANNER

	SUNDAY	MONDAY	TUESDAY

	WEDNESDAY	THURSDAY	FRIDAY	SATURDAY

SUNDAY — MORNING PREPARATION
WEEK 5, DAY 1

DATE:

How long did you sleep?   Meditate ☐ (pg 658)

How well did you sleep? /5   Exercise ☐

Morning Reading:

NOTES:

Review your 7-day goals. With those goals in mind, make a **'Knockout List'** of 3-5 tasks you must work to complete today. Specify the tasks, and make them something you expect you can achieve today.

What are some obstacles you are likely to face today?

What can you do to prepare for or reduce the chances of them happening?

What should you do if these obstacles happen?

> "The impediment to action advances action. What stands in the way becomes the way."
>
> *- Marcus Aurelius*

(See pg 656 for writing prompts)

EVENING REVIEW

BREAKFAST	LUNCH	SUPPER	SNACKS

What were the most significant obstacles you faced today?

How could these obstacles have been worse?

How did you or how can you mitigate these obstacles?

How can you reduce the chances of them reoccurring?

How can these obstacles benefit you?

What mistakes did you make today?

What could you have done that would have been worse?

What can you do to mitigate these mistakes?

What could you do better next time?

What did you do well today?

What can you look forward to tomorrow?

Did you do what was appropriate to complete your tasks?	**YES / NO**
Did you complete your knockout list?	**YES / NO**
Are you closer to your goals today?	**YES / NO**
Did you behave according to your principles?	**YES / NO**

Fill in your Gratitude Log and 28 Day Tracking

Evening Reading:

Meditate ☐
(pg 659)

MONDAY — WEEK 5, DAY 2
MORNING PREPARATION

DATE:

How long did you sleep?   Meditate ☐   Morning Reading:
(pg 658)

How well did you sleep? /5   Exercise ☐

NOTES:

Review your 7-day goals. With those goals in mind, make a **'Knockout List'** of 3-5 tasks you must work to complete today. Specify the tasks, and make them something you expect you can achieve today.

What are some obstacles you are likely to face today?

What can you do to prepare for or reduce the chances of them happening?

What should you do if these obstacles happen?

Don't wait. Seize the day!

(See pg 656 for writing prompts)

EVENING REVIEW

BREAKFAST	LUNCH	SUPPER	SNACKS

What were the most significant obstacles you faced today?

How could these obstacles have been worse?

How did you or how can you mitigate these obstacles?

How can you reduce the chances of them reoccurring?

How can these obstacles benefit you?

What mistakes did you make today?

What could you have done that would have been worse?

What can you do to mitigate these mistakes?

What could you do better next time?

What did you do well today?

What can you look forward to tomorrow?

Did you do what was appropriate to complete your tasks?	**YES / NO**
Did you complete your knockout list?	**YES / NO**
Are you closer to your goals today?	**YES / NO**
Did you behave according to your principles?	**YES / NO**

Fill in your Gratitude Log and 28 Day Tracking

Evening Reading:

Meditate ☐
(pg 659)

TUESDAY — MORNING PREPARATION
WEEK 5, DAY 3

DATE:

How long did you sleep? Meditate ☐ (pg 658)

How well did you sleep? /5 Exercise ☐

Morning Reading:

NOTES:

Review your 7-day goals. With those goals in mind, make a **'Knockout List'** of 3-5 tasks you must work to complete today. Specify the tasks, and make them something you expect you can achieve today.

What are some obstacles you are likely to face today?

What can you do to prepare for or reduce the chances of them happening?

What should you do if these obstacles happen?

Isolate what you have to master, and then master it part by part

(See pg 656 for writing prompts)

EVENING REVIEW

BREAKFAST	LUNCH	SUPPER	SNACKS

What were the most significant obstacles you faced today?

How could these obstacles have been worse?

How did you or how can you mitigate these obstacles?

How can you reduce the chances of them reoccurring?

How can these obstacles benefit you?

What mistakes did you make today?

What could you have done that would have been worse?

What can you do to mitigate these mistakes?

What could you do better next time?

What did you do well today?

What can you look forward to tomorrow?

Did you do what was appropriate to complete your tasks?	**YES / NO**
Did you complete your knockout list?	**YES / NO**
Are you closer to your goals today?	**YES / NO**
Did you behave according to your principles?	**YES / NO**

Fill in your Gratitude Log and 28 Day Tracking

Evening Reading:

Meditate ☐
(pg 659)

WEDNESDAY — MORNING PREPARATION
WEEK 5, DAY 4

DATE:

How long did you sleep? Meditate ☐ (pg 658)

How well did you sleep? /5 Exercise ☐

Morning Reading:

NOTES:

Review your 7-day goals. With those goals in mind, make a **'Knockout List'** of 3-5 tasks you must work to complete today. Specify the tasks, and make them something you expect you can achieve today.

What are some obstacles you are likely to face today?

What can you do to prepare for or reduce the chances of them happening?

What should you do if these obstacles happen?

> "Learn to ask of all actions, "Why are they doing that?" Starting with your own."
>
> *- Marcus Aurelius*

(See pg 656 for writing prompts)

EVENING REVIEW

BREAKFAST	LUNCH	SUPPER	SNACKS

What were the most significant obstacles you faced today?

How could these obstacles have been worse?

How did you or how can you mitigate these obstacles?

How can you reduce the chances of them reoccurring?

How can these obstacles benefit you?

What mistakes did you make today?

What could you have done that would have been worse?

What can you do to mitigate these mistakes?

What could you do better next time?

What did you do well today?

What can you look forward to tomorrow?

Did you do what was appropriate to complete your tasks?	**YES / NO**
Did you complete your knockout list?	**YES / NO**
Are you closer to your goals today?	**YES / NO**
Did you behave according to your principles?	**YES / NO**

Fill in your Gratitude Log and 28 Day Tracking

Evening Reading:

Meditate ☐
(pg 659)

THURSDAY — WEEK 5, DAY 5
MORNING PREPARATION

DATE:

How long did you sleep?   Meditate ☐   Morning Reading:
(pg 658)

How well did you sleep? /5   Exercise ☐

NOTES:

Review your 7-day goals. With those goals in mind, make a '**Knockout List**' of 3-5 tasks you must work to complete today. Specify the tasks, and make them something you expect you can achieve today.

What are some obstacles you are likely to face today?

What can you do to prepare for or reduce the chances of them happening?

What should you do if these obstacles happen?

> Make the best use of what is in your power, and take the rest as it happens. Some things are up to us and some things are not up to us.
>
> - *Epictetus*

(See pg 656 for writing prompts)

EVENING REVIEW

BREAKFAST	LUNCH	SUPPER	SNACKS

What were the most significant obstacles you faced today?

How could these obstacles have been worse?

How did you or how can you mitigate these obstacles?

How can you reduce the chances of them reoccurring?

How can these obstacles benefit you?

What mistakes did you make today?

What could you have done that would have been worse?

What can you do to mitigate these mistakes?

What could you do better next time?

What did you do well today?

What can you look forward to tomorrow?

Did you do what was appropriate to complete your tasks?	**YES / NO**
Did you complete your knockout list?	**YES / NO**
Are you closer to your goals today?	**YES / NO**
Did you behave according to your principles?	**YES / NO**

◯ Fill in your Gratitude Log and 28 Day Tracking

Evening Reading:

Meditate ☐
(pg 659)

FRIDAY
MORNING PREPARATION
WEEK 5, DAY 6

DATE:

How long did you sleep?   Meditate ☐   Morning Reading:
(pg 658)

How well did you sleep? /5   Exercise ☐

NOTES:

Review your 7-day goals. With those goals in mind, make a **'Knockout List'** of 3-5 tasks you must work to complete today. Specify the tasks, and make them something you expect you can achieve today.

What are some obstacles you are likely to face today?

What can you do to prepare for or reduce the chances of them happening?

What should you do if these obstacles happen?

> "Begin at once to live, and count each separate day as a separate life."
> — *Seneca*

(See pg 656 for writing prompts)

EVENTING REVIEW

BREAKFAST	LUNCH	SUPPER	SNACKS

What were the most significant obstacles you faced today?

How could these obstacles have been worse?

How did you or how can you mitigate these obstacles?

How can you reduce the chances of them reoccurring?

How can these obstacles benefit you?

What mistakes did you make today?

What could you have done that would have been worse?

What can you do to mitigate these mistakes?

What could you do better next time?

What did you do well today?

What can you look forward to tomorrow?

Did you do what was appropriate to complete your tasks?	**YES / NO**
Did you complete your knockout list?	**YES / NO**
Are you closer to your goals today?	**YES / NO**
Did you behave according to your principles?	**YES / NO**

Fill in your Gratitude Log and 28 Day Tracking

Evening Reading:

Meditate ☐
(pg 659)

SATURDAY — WEEK 5, DAY 7
MORNING PREPARATION

DATE:

How long did you sleep? Meditate ☐ Morning Reading:
(pg 658)

How well did you sleep? /5 Exercise ☐

NOTES:

Review your 7-day goals. With those goals in mind, make a **'Knockout List'** of 3-5 tasks you must work to complete today. Specify the tasks, and make them something you expect you can achieve today.

What are some obstacles you are likely to face today?

What can you do to prepare for or reduce the chances of them happening?

What should you do if these obstacles happen?

Keep pressing on.

(See pg 656 for writing prompts)

EVENING REVIEW

BREAKFAST	LUNCH	SUPPER	SNACKS

What were the most significant obstacles you faced today?

How could these obstacles have been worse?

How did you or how can you mitigate these obstacles?

How can you reduce the chances of them reoccurring?

How can these obstacles benefit you?

What mistakes did you make today?

What could you have done that would have been worse?

What can you do to mitigate these mistakes?

What could you do better next time?

What did you do well today?

What can you look forward to tomorrow?

Did you do what was appropriate to complete your tasks?	YES / NO
Did you complete your knockout list?	YES / NO
Are you closer to your goals today?	YES / NO
Did you behave according to your principles?	YES / NO

Fill in your Gratitude Log and 28 Day Tracking

Evening Reading:

Meditate ☐
(pg 659)

WEEK 5 GRATITUDE LOG

Write briefly about anything that you have to be grateful for for each day.

If you are having difficulty thinking about what to write, you can consult the prompts on page 657.

SUNDAY

MONDAY

TUESDAY

WEDNESDAY

THURSDAY

FRIDAY

SATURDAY

WEEKLY PREMEDITATION OF OBSTACLES

Think of a significant obstacle happening to you, or think about suffering a significant loss. Imagine it as if it were happening now. Describe it in detail.

What would be the best way to react to this happening?

What are some things you now enjoy which you could no longer enjoy if this happens to you? Describe what you enjoy about it in detail.

How could you repair any damage caused if this happened?

What could you still enjoy in your life if this happened?

What could you do to prepare for or reduce the chances of this happening?

It's a possibility that this could happen to you. But it hasn't yet. What can you do to appreciate what you have now?

WEEK 5 REVIEW

Review your 7-day goals. Did you accomplish them? **YES / NO**
If no, consider why not, and if it is still worth your time. If it is, migrate it forward into a future task.

What were the best things that happened this week?

Which activities did not work well for you this week?

What activities worked well for you this week?

Overall, this week was:

7-DAY GOAL SETTING - WEEK 6

Review your 28 day goals. Consider the steps you should do to achieve the goals, and what you can do to reduce the chances of the obstacles you anticipated. With those in mind, what are your goals for the next 7 days? Make them specific and achievable in 7 days.

Why are these steps important?

What part of these steps are in your control?

WEEKLY THEME

Adapt to your circumstances

WEEKLY REFLECTION

(See pg 656 for writing prompts)

291

WEEK 6 PLANNER

	SUNDAY	MONDAY	TUESDAY

	WEDNESDAY	THURSDAY	FRIDAY	SATURDAY

SUNDAY — WEEK 6, DAY 1
MORNING PREPARATION

DATE:

How long did you sleep?　　　Meditate ☐
(pg 658)

How well did you sleep?　/5　Exercise ☐

Morning Reading:

NOTES:

Review your 7-day goals. With those goals in mind, make a **'Knockout List'** of 3-5 tasks you must work to complete today. Specify the tasks, and make them something you expect you can achieve today.

What are some obstacles you are likely to face today?

What can you do to prepare for or reduce the chances of them happening?

What should you do if these obstacles happen?

> "Everything's destiny is to change, to be transformed, to perish. So that new things can be born.."
>
> *- Marcus Aurelius*

(See pg 656 for writing prompts)

EVENING REVIEW

BREAKFAST	LUNCH	SUPPER	SNACKS

What were the most significant obstacles you faced today?

How could these obstacles have been worse?

How did you or how can you mitigate these obstacles?

How can you reduce the chances of them reoccurring?

How can these obstacles benefit you?

What mistakes did you make today?

What could you have done that would have been worse?

What can you do to mitigate these mistakes?

What could you do better next time?

What did you do well today?

What can you look forward to tomorrow?

Did you do what was appropriate to complete your tasks?	**YES / NO**
Did you complete your knockout list?	**YES / NO**
Are you closer to your goals today?	**YES / NO**
Did you behave according to your principles?	**YES / NO**

Fill in your Gratitude Log and 28 Day Tracking

Evening Reading:

Meditate ☐
(pg 659)

MONDAY — WEEK 6, DAY 2
MORNING PREPARATION

DATE:

How long did you sleep?   Meditate ☐   Morning Reading:
(pg 658)

How well did you sleep? /5   Exercise ☐

NOTES:

Review your 7-day goals. With those goals in mind, make a **'Knockout List'** of 3-5 tasks you must work to complete today. Specify the tasks, and make them something you expect you can achieve today.

What are some obstacles you are likely to face today?

What can you do to prepare for or reduce the chances of them happening?

What should you do if these obstacles happen?

> **The past has determined where you are.
> You can determine what you will do next.**

(See pg 656 for writing prompts)

EVENING REVIEW

BREAKFAST	LUNCH	SUPPER	SNACKS

What were the most significant obstacles you faced today?

How could these obstacles have been worse?

How did you or how can you mitigate these obstacles?

How can you reduce the chances of them reoccurring?

How can these obstacles benefit you?

What mistakes did you make today?

What could you have done that would have been worse?

What can you do to mitigate these mistakes?

What could you do better next time?

What did you do well today?

What can you look forward to tomorrow?

Did you do what was appropriate to complete your tasks?	**YES / NO**
Did you complete your knockout list?	**YES / NO**
Are you closer to your goals today?	**YES / NO**
Did you behave according to your principles?	**YES / NO**

◯ Fill in your Gratitude Log and 28 Day Tracking

Evening Reading:

Meditate ☐
(pg 659)

TUESDAY — WEEK 6, DAY 3
MORNING PREPARATION

DATE:

How long did you sleep?　　Meditate ☐　　Morning Reading:
(pg 658)

How well did you sleep?　/5　Exercise ☐

NOTES:

Review your 7-day goals. With those goals in mind, make a **'Knockout List'** of 3-5 tasks you must work to complete today. Specify the tasks, and make them something you expect you can achieve today.

What are some obstacles you are likely to face today?

What can you do to prepare for or reduce the chances of them happening?

What should you do if these obstacles happen?

> "The first rule is to keep an untroubled spirit. The second is to look things in the face and know them for what they are."
> — *Marcus Aurelius*

(See pg 656 for writing prompts)

EVENING REVIEW

BREAKFAST	LUNCH	SUPPER	SNACKS

What were the most significant obstacles you faced today?

How could these obstacles have been worse?

How did you or how can you mitigate these obstacles?

How can you reduce the chances of them reoccurring?

How can these obstacles benefit you?

What mistakes did you make today?

What could you have done that would have been worse?

What can you do to mitigate these mistakes?

What could you do better next time?

What did you do well today?

What can you look forward to tomorrow?

Did you do what was appropriate to complete your tasks?	**YES / NO**
Did you complete your knockout list?	**YES / NO**
Are you closer to your goals today?	**YES / NO**
Did you behave according to your principles?	**YES / NO**

◯ Fill in your Gratitude Log and 28 Day Tracking

Evening Reading:

Meditate ☐
(pg 659)

WEDNESDAY — MORNING PREPARATION
WEEK 6, DAY 4

DATE:

How long did you sleep?　　Meditate ☐　　Morning Reading:
(pg 658)

How well did you sleep?　/5　Exercise ☐

NOTES:

Review your 7-day goals. With those goals in mind, make a **'Knockout List'** of 3-5 tasks you must work to complete today. Specify the tasks, and make them something you expect you can achieve today.

What are some obstacles you are likely to face today?

What can you do to prepare for or reduce the chances of them happening?

What should you do if these obstacles happen?

> "Will I not walk in the footsteps of my predecessors? I will indeed use the ancient road - but if I find another route that is more direct and has fewer ups and downs, I will stake out that one."
>
> *- Seneca*

(See pg 656 for writing prompts)

EVENTING REVIEW

BREAKFAST	LUNCH	SUPPER	SNACKS

What were the most significant obstacles you faced today?

How could these obstacles have been worse?

How did you or how can you mitigate these obstacles?

How can you reduce the chances of them reoccurring?

How can these obstacles benefit you?

What mistakes did you make today?

What could you have done that would have been worse?

What can you do to mitigate these mistakes?

What could you do better next time?

What did you do well today?

What can you look forward to tomorrow?

Did you do what was appropriate to complete your tasks?	**YES / NO**
Did you complete your knockout list?	**YES / NO**
Are you closer to your goals today?	**YES / NO**
Did you behave according to your principles?	**YES / NO**

Fill in your Gratitude Log and 28 Day Tracking

Evening Reading:

Meditate ☐
(pg 659)

THURSDAY — WEEK 6, DAY 5
MORNING PREPARATION

DATE:

How long did you sleep?   Meditate ☐   (pg 658)

How well did you sleep? /5   Exercise ☐

Morning Reading:

NOTES:

Review your 7-day goals. With those goals in mind, make a **'Knockout List'** of 3-5 tasks you must work to complete today. Specify the tasks, and make them something you expect you can achieve today.

What are some obstacles you are likely to face today?

What can you do to prepare for or reduce the chances of them happening?

What should you do if these obstacles happen?

Everything changes, nothing dies

- Ovid

(See pg 656 for writing prompts)

EVENING REVIEW

BREAKFAST	LUNCH	SUPPER	SNACKS

What were the most significant obstacles you faced today?

How could these obstacles have been worse?

How did you or how can you mitigate these obstacles?

How can you reduce the chances of them reoccurring?

How can these obstacles benefit you?

What mistakes did you make today?

What could you have done that would have been worse?

What can you do to mitigate these mistakes?

What could you do better next time?

What did you do well today?

What can you look forward to tomorrow?

Did you do what was appropriate to complete your tasks?	**YES / NO**
Did you complete your knockout list?	**YES / NO**
Are you closer to your goals today?	**YES / NO**
Did you behave according to your principles?	**YES / NO**

◯ Fill in your Gratitude Log and 28 Day Tracking

Evening Reading:

Meditate ☐
(pg 659)

FRIDAY — WEEK 6, DAY 6
MORNING PREPARATION

DATE:

How long did you sleep?   Meditate ☐   Morning Reading:
(pg 658)

How well did you sleep? /5   Exercise ☐

NOTES:

Review your 7-day goals. With those goals in mind, make a **'Knockout List'** of 3-5 tasks you must work to complete today. Specify the tasks, and make them something you expect you can achieve today.

What are some obstacles you are likely to face today?

What can you do to prepare for or reduce the chances of them happening?

What should you do if these obstacles happen?

> "Change Your Thoughts and you'll change the world"
>
> *– Marcus Aurelius*

(See pg 656 for writing prompts)

EVENING REVIEW

BREAKFAST	LUNCH	SUPPER	SNACKS

What were the most significant obstacles you faced today?

How could these obstacles have been worse?

How did you or how can you mitigate these obstacles?

How can you reduce the chances of them reoccurring?

How can these obstacles benefit you?

What mistakes did you make today?

What could you have done that would have been worse?

What can you do to mitigate these mistakes?

What could you do better next time?

What did you do well today?

What can you look forward to tomorrow?

Did you do what was appropriate to complete your tasks?	**YES / NO**
Did you complete your knockout list?	**YES / NO**
Are you closer to your goals today?	**YES / NO**
Did you behave according to your principles?	**YES / NO**

Fill in your Gratitude Log and 28 Day Tracking

Evening Reading:

Meditate ☐
(pg 659)

SATURDAY — MORNING PREPARATION
WEEK 6, DAY 7

DATE:

How long did you sleep? Meditate ☐   Morning Reading:
(pg 658)

How well did you sleep? /5   Exercise ☐

NOTES:

Review your 7-day goals. With those goals in mind, make a **'Knockout List'** of 3-5 tasks you must work to complete today. Specify the tasks, and make them something you expect you can achieve today.

What are some obstacles you are likely to face today?

What can you do to prepare for or reduce the chances of them happening?

What should you do if these obstacles happen?

> **The times change, and we change with them.**

(See pg 656 for writing prompts)

EVENING REVIEW

BREAKFAST	LUNCH	SUPPER	SNACKS

What were the most significant obstacles you faced today?

How could these obstacles have been worse?

How did you or how can you mitigate these obstacles?

How can you reduce the chances of them reoccurring?

How can these obstacles benefit you?

What mistakes did you make today?

What could you have done that would have been worse?

What can you do to mitigate these mistakes?

What could you do better next time?

What did you do well today?

What can you look forward to tomorrow?

Did you do what was appropriate to complete your tasks?	**YES / NO**
Did you complete your knockout list?	**YES / NO**
Are you closer to your goals today?	**YES / NO**
Did you behave according to your principles?	**YES / NO**

Fill in your Gratitude Log and 28 Day Tracking

Evening Reading:

Meditate ☐
(pg 659)

WEEK 6 GRATITUDE LOG

Write briefly about anything that you have to be grateful for for each day.

If you are having difficulty thinking about what to write, you can consult the prompts on page 657.

SUNDAY

MONDAY

TUESDAY

WEDNESDAY

THURSDAY

FRIDAY

SATURDAY

WEEKLY PREMEDITATION OF OBSTACLES

Think of a significant obstacle happening to you, or think about suffering a significant loss. Imagine it as if it were happening now. Describe it in detail.

What would be the best way to react to this happening?

What are some things you now enjoy which you could no longer enjoy if this happens to you? Describe what you enjoy about it in detail.

How could you repair any damage caused if this happened?

What could you still enjoy in your life if this happened?

What could you do to prepare for or reduce the chances of this happening?

It's a possibility that this could happen to you. But it hasn't yet. What can you do to appreciate what you have now?

WEEK 6 REVIEW

○ Review your 7-day goals. Did you accomplish them? **YES / NO**
If no, consider why not, and if it is still worth your time. If it is, migrate it forward into a future task.

What were the best things that happened this week?

Which activities did not work well for you this week?

What activities worked well for you this week?

Overall, this week was:

7-DAY GOAL SETTING - WEEK 7

Review your 28 day goals. Consider the steps you should do to achieve the goals, and what you can do to reduce the chances of the obstacles you anticipated. With those in mind, what are your goals for the next 7 days? Make them specific and achievable in 7 days.

Why are these steps important?

What part of these steps are in your control?

331

WEEKLY THEME

Everything is connected

WEEKLY REFLECTION

(See pg 656 for writing prompts)

335

WEEK 7 PLANNER

	SUNDAY	MONDAY	TUESDAY

	WEDNESDAY	THURSDAY	FRIDAY	SATURDAY

SUNDAY — WEEK 7, DAY 1
MORNING PREPARATION

DATE:

How long did you sleep?   Meditate ☐   Morning Reading:
(pg 658)

How well did you sleep? /5   Exercise ☐

NOTES:

Review your 7-day goals. With those goals in mind, make a **'Knockout List'** of 3-5 tasks you must work to complete today. Specify the tasks, and make them something you expect you can achieve today.

What are some obstacles you are likely to face today?

What can you do to prepare for or reduce the chances of them happening?

What should you do if these obstacles happen?

"Honor the highest thing in the Universe; it is the power on which all things depend; it is the light by which all of life is guided."

- Marcus Aurelius

(See pg 656 for writing prompts)

EVENING REVIEW

BREAKFAST	LUNCH	SUPPER	SNACKS

What were the most significant obstacles you faced today?

How could these obstacles have been worse?

How did you or how can you mitigate these obstacles?

How can you reduce the chances of them reoccurring?

How can these obstacles benefit you?

What mistakes did you make today?

What could you have done that would have been worse?

What can you do to mitigate these mistakes?

What could you do better next time?

What did you do well today?

What can you look forward to tomorrow?

Did you do what was appropriate to complete your tasks?	**YES / NO**
Did you complete your knockout list?	**YES / NO**
Are you closer to your goals today?	**YES / NO**
Did you behave according to your principles?	**YES / NO**

○ Fill in your Gratitude Log and 28 Day Tracking

Evening Reading:

Meditate ☐
(pg 659)

MONDAY — WEEK 7, DAY 2
MORNING PREPARATION

DATE:

How long did you sleep?   Meditate ☐   Morning Reading:
(pg 658)

How well did you sleep? /5   Exercise ☐

NOTES:

Review your 7-day goals. With those goals in mind, make a **'Knockout List'** of 3-5 tasks you must work to complete today. Specify the tasks, and make them something you expect you can achieve today.

What are some obstacles you are likely to face today?

What can you do to prepare for or reduce the chances of them happening?

What should you do if these obstacles happen?

"Constantly regard the universe as one living being, having one substance and one soul; and observe how all things have reference to one perception, the perception of this one living being; and how all things act with one movement; and how all things are the cooperating causes of all things that exist; observe too the continuous spinning of the thread and the structure of the web."

- Marcus Aurelius

(See pg 656 for writing prompts)

EVENING REVIEW

BREAKFAST	LUNCH	SUPPER	SNACKS

What were the most significant obstacles you faced today?

How could these obstacles have been worse?

How did you or how can you mitigate these obstacles?

How can you reduce the chances of them reoccurring?

How can these obstacles benefit you?

What mistakes did you make today?

What could you have done that would have been worse?

What can you do to mitigate these mistakes?

What could you do better next time?

What did you do well today?

What can you look forward to tomorrow?

Did you do what was appropriate to complete your tasks?	**YES / NO**
Did you complete your knockout list?	**YES / NO**
Are you closer to your goals today?	**YES / NO**
Did you behave according to your principles?	**YES / NO**

Fill in your Gratitude Log and 28 Day Tracking

Evening Reading:

Meditate ☐
(pg 659)

TUESDAY — MORNING PREPARATION
WEEK 7, DAY 3

DATE:

How long did you sleep?   Meditate ☐   Morning Reading:
(pg 658)

How well did you sleep? /5   Exercise ☐

NOTES:

Review your 7-day goals. With those goals in mind, make a **'Knockout List'** of 3-5 tasks you must work to complete today. Specify the tasks, and make them something you expect you can achieve today.

What are some obstacles you are likely to face today?

What can you do to prepare for or reduce the chances of them happening?

What should you do if these obstacles happen?

> "Just as ripples spread out when a single pebble is dropped into water, the actions of individuals can have far-reaching effects."
>
> *- Dalai Lama*

(See pg 656 for writing prompts)

EVENING REVIEW

BREAKFAST	LUNCH	SUPPER	SNACKS

What were the most significant obstacles you faced today?

How could these obstacles have been worse?

How did you or how can you mitigate these obstacles?

How can you reduce the chances of them reoccurring?

How can these obstacles benefit you?

What mistakes did you make today?

What could you have done that would have been worse?

What can you do to mitigate these mistakes?

What could you do better next time?

What did you do well today?

What can you look forward to tomorrow?

Did you do what was appropriate to complete your tasks?	**YES / NO**
Did you complete your knockout list?	**YES / NO**
Are you closer to your goals today?	**YES / NO**
Did you behave according to your principles?	**YES / NO**

Fill in your Gratitude Log and 28 Day Tracking

Evening Reading:

Meditate ☐
(pg 659)

WEDNESDAY — WEEK 7, DAY 4
MORNING PREPARATION

DATE:

How long did you sleep?   Meditate ☐   Morning Reading:
(pg 658)

How well did you sleep? /5   Exercise ☐

NOTES:

Review your 7-day goals. With those goals in mind, make a **'Knockout List'** of 3-5 tasks you must work to complete today. Specify the tasks, and make them something you expect you can achieve today.

What are some obstacles you are likely to face today?

What can you do to prepare for or reduce the chances of them happening?

What should you do if these obstacles happen?

> "Whatever happens to you has been waiting to happen since the beginning of time."
>
> *- Marcus Aurelius*

(See pg 656 for writing prompts)

EVENING REVIEW

BREAKFAST	LUNCH	SUPPER	SNACKS

What were the most significant obstacles you faced today?

How could these obstacles have been worse?

How did you or how can you mitigate these obstacles?

How can you reduce the chances of them reoccurring?

How can these obstacles benefit you?

What mistakes did you make today?

What could you have done that would have been worse?

What can you do to mitigate these mistakes?

What could you do better next time?

What did you do well today?

What can you look forward to tomorrow?

Did you do what was appropriate to complete your tasks?	**YES / NO**
Did you complete your knockout list?	**YES / NO**
Are you closer to your goals today?	**YES / NO**
Did you behave according to your principles?	**YES / NO**

◯ Fill in your Gratitude Log and 28 Day Tracking

Evening Reading:

Meditate ☐
(pg 659)

THURSDAY — WEEK 7, DAY 5
MORNING PREPARATION

DATE:

How long did you sleep? Meditate ☐ Morning Reading:
(pg 658)

How well did you sleep? /5 Exercise ☐

NOTES:

Review your 7-day goals. With those goals in mind, make a **'Knockout List'** of 3-5 tasks you must work to complete today. Specify the tasks, and make them something you expect you can achieve today.

What are some obstacles you are likely to face today?

What can you do to prepare for or reduce the chances of them happening?

What should you do if these obstacles happen?

> "Every part of me then will be reduced by change into some part of the universe, and that again will change into another part of the universe, and so on forever."
> - *Marcus Aurelius*

(See pg 656 for writing prompts)

EVENING REVIEW

BREAKFAST	LUNCH	SUPPER	SNACKS

What were the most significant obstacles you faced today?

How could these obstacles have been worse?

How did you or how can you mitigate these obstacles?

How can you reduce the chances of them reoccurring?

How can these obstacles benefit you?

What mistakes did you make today?

What could you have done that would have been worse?

What can you do to mitigate these mistakes?

What could you do better next time?

What did you do well today?

What can you look forward to tomorrow?

Did you do what was appropriate to complete your tasks?	**YES / NO**
Did you complete your knockout list?	**YES / NO**
Are you closer to your goals today?	**YES / NO**
Did you behave according to your principles?	**YES / NO**

Fill in your Gratitude Log and 28 Day Tracking

Evening Reading:

Meditate ☐
(pg 659)

FRIDAY
MORNING PREPARATION
WEEK 7, DAY 6

DATE:

How long did you sleep?   Meditate ☐ (pg 658)

How well did you sleep? /5   Exercise ☐

Morning Reading:

NOTES:

Review your 7-day goals. With those goals in mind, make a **'Knockout List'** of 3-5 tasks you must work to complete today. Specify the tasks, and make them something you expect you can achieve today.

What are some obstacles you are likely to face today?

What can you do to prepare for or reduce the chances of them happening?

What should you do if these obstacles happen?

> "All things are parts of one single system, which is called nature; the individual life is good when it is in harmony with nature."
>
> *- Zeno of Citium*

(See pg 656 for writing prompts)

EVENTING REVIEW

BREAKFAST	LUNCH	SUPPER	SNACKS

What were the most significant obstacles you faced today?

How could these obstacles have been worse?

How did you or how can you mitigate these obstacles?

How can you reduce the chances of them reoccurring?

How can these obstacles benefit you?

What mistakes did you make today?

What could you have done that would have been worse?

What can you do to mitigate these mistakes?

What could you do better next time?

What did you do well today?

What can you look forward to tomorrow?

Did you do what was appropriate to complete your tasks?	**YES / NO**
Did you complete your knockout list?	**YES / NO**
Are you closer to your goals today?	**YES / NO**
Did you behave according to your principles?	**YES / NO**

Fill in your Gratitude Log and 28 Day Tracking

Evening Reading:

Meditate ☐
(pg 659)

SATURDAY — WEEK 7, DAY 7
MORNING PREPARATION

DATE:

How long did you sleep? Meditate ☐
(pg 658)

How well did you sleep? /5 Exercise ☐

Morning Reading:

NOTES:

Review your 7-day goals. With those goals in mind, make a **'Knockout List'** of 3-5 tasks you must work to complete today. Specify the tasks, and make them something you expect you can achieve today.

What are some obstacles you are likely to face today?

What can you do to prepare for or reduce the chances of them happening?

What should you do if these obstacles happen?

"Whether the universe is a concourse of atoms, or nature is a system, let this first be established: that I am a part of the whole that is governed by nature; next, that I stand in some intimate connection with other kindred parts."

- Marcus Aurelius

(See pg 656 for writing prompts)

EVENING REVIEW

BREAKFAST	LUNCH	SUPPER	SNACKS

What were the most significant obstacles you faced today?

How could these obstacles have been worse?

How did you or how can you mitigate these obstacles?

How can you reduce the chances of them reoccurring?

How can these obstacles benefit you?

What mistakes did you make today?

What could you have done that would have been worse?

What can you do to mitigate these mistakes?

What could you do better next time?

What did you do well today?

What can you look forward to tomorrow?

Did you do what was appropriate to complete your tasks?	**YES / NO**
Did you complete your knockout list?	**YES / NO**
Are you closer to your goals today?	**YES / NO**
Did you behave according to your principles?	**YES / NO**

Fill in your Gratitude Log and 28 Day Tracking

Evening Reading:

Meditate ☐
(pg 659)

366

WEEK 7 GRATITUDE LOG

Write briefly about anything that you have to be grateful for for each day.

If you are having difficulty thinking about what to write, you can consult the prompts on page 657.

SUNDAY

MONDAY

TUESDAY

WEDNESDAY

THURSDAY

FRIDAY

SATURDAY

MEMENTO MORI REFLECTION
Remember, you will die.

It is inevitable that you will die. How have you accepted that fact?

How would a terminal illness or anything that would foreshadow the end of your life change how you think you would live today?

You can't take anything with you. What are some things that you value that ultimately won't matter once you're dead?

What are some things you have been worrying about? If you were to learn you would die tomorrow would you still worry about them?

What are things you should cherish more knowing your time is limited?

There are countless ways to die. Imagine a way you could die and describe it here.

Death is not the end. Everything changes. Nothing perishes. Every part of you will be reduced by change into some part of the universe, and that again will change into another part of the universe, and so on forever. How does this affect your thoughts on death?

Our actions echo beyond their immediate effects. How we live will continue to affect the world even after we die. How will the way you've lived affect the world after you die? How do you want it to?

Remember to live. You aren't guaranteed any length of life. Don't act like you will live forever. What do you want to get done while you are alive? Your time is already flying. Seize the day!

WEEK 7 REVIEW

○ Review your 7-day goals. Did you accomplish them? **YES / NO**
If no, consider why not, and if it is still worth your time. If it is, migrate it forward into a future task.

What were the best things that happened this week?

Which activities did not work well for you this week?

What activities worked well for you this week?

Overall, this week was:

7-DAY GOAL SETTING - WEEK 8

Review your 28 day goals. Consider the steps you should do to achieve the goals, and what you can do to reduce the chances of the obstacles you anticipated. With those in mind, what are your goals for the next 7 days? Make them specific and achievable in 7 days.

Why are these steps important?

What part of these steps are in your control?

374

WEEKLY THEME

Mutual Benefit

WEEKLY REFLECTION

(See pg 656 for writing prompts)

WEEK 8 PLANNER

	SUNDAY	MONDAY	TUESDAY

	WEDNESDAY	THURSDAY	FRIDAY	SATURDAY

SUNDAY — WEEK 8, DAY 1
MORNING PREPARATION

DATE:

How long did you sleep?   Meditate ☐   Morning Reading:
(pg 658)
How well did you sleep? /5   Exercise ☐

NOTES:

Review your 7-day goals. With those goals in mind, make a **'Knockout List'** of 3-5 tasks you must work to complete today. Specify the tasks, and make them something you expect you can achieve today.

What are some obstacles you are likely to face today?

What can you do to prepare for or reduce the chances of them happening?

What should you do if these obstacles happen?

> "Nature bore us related to one another ... She instilled in us a mutual love and made us compatible ... Let us hold everything in common; we stem from a common source. Our fellowship is very similar to an arch of stones, which would fall apart, if they did not reciprocally support each other."
>
> *- Marcus Aurelius*

(See pg 656 for writing prompts)

EVENING REVIEW

BREAKFAST	LUNCH	SUPPER	SNACKS

What were the most significant obstacles you faced today?

How could these obstacles have been worse?

How did you or how can you mitigate these obstacles?

How can you reduce the chances of them reoccurring?

How can these obstacles benefit you?

What mistakes did you make today?

What could you have done that would have been worse?

What can you do to mitigate these mistakes?

What could you do better next time?

What did you do well today?

What can you look forward to tomorrow?

Did you do what was appropriate to complete your tasks?	**YES / NO**
Did you complete your knockout list?	**YES / NO**
Are you closer to your goals today?	**YES / NO**
Did you behave according to your principles?	**YES / NO**

Fill in your Gratitude Log and 28 Day Tracking

Evening Reading:

Meditate ☐
(pg 659)

MONDAY — WEEK 8, DAY 2
MORNING PREPARATION

DATE:

How long did you sleep?   Meditate ☐   Morning Reading:
(pg 658)

How well did you sleep? /5   Exercise ☐

NOTES:

Review your 7-day goals. With those goals in mind, make a **'Knockout List'** of 3-5 tasks you must work to complete today. Specify the tasks, and make them something you expect you can achieve today.

What are some obstacles you are likely to face today?

What can you do to prepare for or reduce the chances of them happening?

What should you do if these obstacles happen?

"The universe made rational creatures for the sake of each other, with an eye toward mutual benefit based on true value and never for harm.."

- Marcus Aurelius

(See pg 656 for writing prompts)

EVENING REVIEW

BREAKFAST	LUNCH	SUPPER	SNACKS

What were the most significant obstacles you faced today?

How could these obstacles have been worse?

How did you or how can you mitigate these obstacles?

How can you reduce the chances of them reoccurring?

How can these obstacles benefit you?

What mistakes did you make today?

What could you have done that would have been worse?

What can you do to mitigate these mistakes?

What could you do better next time?

What did you do well today?

What can you look forward to tomorrow?

Did you do what was appropriate to complete your tasks?	**YES / NO**
Did you complete your knockout list?	**YES / NO**
Are you closer to your goals today?	**YES / NO**
Did you behave according to your principles?	**YES / NO**

Fill in your Gratitude Log and 28 Day Tracking

Evening Reading:

Meditate ☐
(pg 659)

TUESDAY — MORNING PREPARATION
WEEK 8, DAY 3

DATE:

How long did you sleep?   Meditate ☐ (pg 658)

How well did you sleep? /5   Exercise ☐

Morning Reading:

NOTES:

Review your 7-day goals. With those goals in mind, make a **'Knockout List'** of 3-5 tasks you must work to complete today. Specify the tasks, and make them something you expect you can achieve today.

What are some obstacles you are likely to face today?

What can you do to prepare for or reduce the chances of them happening?

What should you do if these obstacles happen?

> "Human beings have been made for the sake of one another. Teach them or endure them."
>
> *- Marcus Aurelius*

(See pg 656 for writing prompts)

EVENING REVIEW

BREAKFAST	LUNCH	SUPPER	SNACKS

What were the most significant obstacles you faced today?

How could these obstacles have been worse?

How did you or how can you mitigate these obstacles?

How can you reduce the chances of them reoccurring?

How can these obstacles benefit you?

What mistakes did you make today?

What could you have done that would have been worse?

What can you do to mitigate these mistakes?

What could you do better next time?

What did you do well today?

What can you look forward to tomorrow?

Did you do what was appropriate to complete your tasks?	**YES / NO**
Did you complete your knockout list?	**YES / NO**
Are you closer to your goals today?	**YES / NO**
Did you behave according to your principles?	**YES / NO**

◯ Fill in your Gratitude Log and 28 Day Tracking

Evening Reading:

Meditate ☐
(pg 659)

WEDNESDAY   WEEK 8, DAY 4
MORNING PREPARATION

DATE:

How long did you sleep?   Meditate ☐   Morning Reading:
(pg 658)

How well did you sleep? /5   Exercise ☐

NOTES:

Review your 7-day goals. With those goals in mind, make a **'Knockout List'** of 3-5 tasks you must work to complete today. Specify the tasks, and make them something you expect you can achieve today.

What are some obstacles you are likely to face today?

What can you do to prepare for or reduce the chances of them happening?

What should you do if these obstacles happen?

> "Let us give in the way in which we ourselves should like to receive."
>
> *- Marcus Aurelius*

(See pg 656 for writing prompts)

EVENING REVIEW

BREAKFAST	LUNCH	SUPPER	SNACKS

What were the most significant obstacles you faced today?

How could these obstacles have been worse?

How did you or how can you mitigate these obstacles?

How can you reduce the chances of them reoccurring?

How can these obstacles benefit you?

What mistakes did you make today?

What could you have done that would have been worse?

What can you do to mitigate these mistakes?

What could you do better next time?

What did you do well today?

What can you look forward to tomorrow?

Did you do what was appropriate to complete your tasks?	**YES / NO**
Did you complete your knockout list?	**YES / NO**
Are you closer to your goals today?	**YES / NO**
Did you behave according to your principles?	**YES / NO**

◯ Fill in your Gratitude Log and 28 Day Tracking

Evening Reading:

Meditate ☐
(pg 659)

THURSDAY — WEEK 8, DAY 5
MORNING PREPARATION

DATE:

How long did you sleep? Meditate ☐ Morning Reading:
(pg 658)

How well did you sleep? /5 Exercise ☐

NOTES:

Review your 7-day goals. With those goals in mind, make a **'Knockout List'** of 3-5 tasks you must work to complete today. Specify the tasks, and make them something you expect you can achieve today.

What are some obstacles you are likely to face today?

What can you do to prepare for or reduce the chances of them happening?

What should you do if these obstacles happen?

"It is a wise thing to be polite; consequently, it is a stupid thing to be rude. To make enemies by unnecessary and willful incivility, is just as insane a proceeding as to set your house on fire."
- *Marcus Aurelius*

(See pg 656 for writing prompts)

EVENING REVIEW

BREAKFAST	LUNCH	SUPPER	SNACKS

What were the most significant obstacles you faced today?

How could these obstacles have been worse?

How did you or how can you mitigate these obstacles?

How can you reduce the chances of them reoccurring?

How can these obstacles benefit you?

What mistakes did you make today?

What could you have done that would have been worse?

What can you do to mitigate these mistakes?

What could you do better next time?

What did you do well today?

What can you look forward to tomorrow?

Did you do what was appropriate to complete your tasks?	**YES / NO**
Did you complete your knockout list?	**YES / NO**
Are you closer to your goals today?	**YES / NO**
Did you behave according to your principles?	**YES / NO**

Fill in your Gratitude Log and 28 Day Tracking

Evening Reading:

Meditate ☐
(pg 659)

FRIDAY — WEEK 8, DAY 6
MORNING PREPARATION

DATE:

How long did you sleep?   Meditate ☐   Morning Reading:
(pg 658)

How well did you sleep? /5   Exercise ☐

NOTES:

Review your 7-day goals. With those goals in mind, make a **'Knockout List'** of 3-5 tasks you must work to complete today. Specify the tasks, and make them something you expect you can achieve today.

What are some obstacles you are likely to face today?

What can you do to prepare for or reduce the chances of them happening?

What should you do if these obstacles happen?

> ## "Abstain from sexual misconduct."
>
> *- 3rd Precept of Buddhism*

(See pg 656 for writing prompts)

EVENING REVIEW

BREAKFAST	LUNCH	SUPPER	SNACKS

What were the most significant obstacles you faced today?

How could these obstacles have been worse?

How did you or how can you mitigate these obstacles?

How can you reduce the chances of them reoccurring?

How can these obstacles benefit you?

What mistakes did you make today?

What could you have done that would have been worse?

What can you do to mitigate these mistakes?

What could you do better next time?

What did you do well today?

What can you look forward to tomorrow?

Did you do what was appropriate to complete your tasks?	**YES / NO**
Did you complete your knockout list?	**YES / NO**
Are you closer to your goals today?	**YES / NO**
Did you behave according to your principles?	**YES / NO**

Fill in your Gratitude Log and 28 Day Tracking

Evening Reading:

Meditate ☐
(pg 659)

SATURDAY
MORNING PREPARATION
WEEK 8, DAY 7

DATE:

How long did you sleep? Meditate ☐ Morning Reading:
(pg 658)

How well did you sleep? /5 Exercise ☐

NOTES:

Review your 7-day goals. With those goals in mind, make a **'Knockout List'** of 3-5 tasks you must work to complete today. Specify the tasks, and make them something you expect you can achieve today.

What are some obstacles you are likely to face today?

What can you do to prepare for or reduce the chances of them happening?

What should you do if these obstacles happen?

> "If it is not right, do not do it, if it is not true, do not say it."
>
> *- Marcus Aurelius*

(See pg 656 for writing prompts)

EVENING REVIEW

BREAKFAST	LUNCH	SUPPER	SNACKS

What were the most significant obstacles you faced today?

How could these obstacles have been worse?

How did you or how can you mitigate these obstacles?

How can you reduce the chances of them reoccurring?

How can these obstacles benefit you?

What mistakes did you make today?

What could you have done that would have been worse?

What can you do to mitigate these mistakes?

What could you do better next time?

What did you do well today?

What can you look forward to tomorrow?

Did you do what was appropriate to complete your tasks?	**YES / NO**
Did you complete your knockout list?	**YES / NO**
Are you closer to your goals today?	**YES / NO**
Did you behave according to your principles?	**YES / NO**

◯ Fill in your Gratitude Log and 28 Day Tracking

Evening Reading:

Meditate ☐
(pg 659)

WEEK 8 GRATITUDE LOG

Write briefly about anything that you have to be grateful for for each day.

If you are having difficulty thinking about what to write, you can consult the prompts on page 657.

SUNDAY

MONDAY

TUESDAY

WEDNESDAY

THURSDAY

FRIDAY

SATURDAY

WEEKLY PREMEDITATION OF OBSTACLES

Think of a significant obstacle happening to you, or think about suffering a significant loss. Imagine it as if it were happening now. Describe it in detail.

What would be the best way to react to this happening?

What are some things you now enjoy which you could no longer enjoy if this happens to you? Describe what you enjoy about it in detail.

How could you repair any damage caused if this happened?

What could you still enjoy in your life if this happened?

What could you do to prepare for or reduce the chances of this happening?

It's a possibility that this could happen to you. But it hasn't yet. What can you do to appreciate what you have now?

28 DAY TRACKING - WEEKS 5-8

HEALTH & WELLNESS REVIEW - WEEKS 5-8

	CURRENT	CHANGE	TARGET
Weight			
Body Fat %			
Neck			
Shoulders			
Chest			
Right Bicep			
Left Bicep			
Right Forearm			
Left Forearm			
Waist			
Hips			
Right Thigh			
Left Thigh			
Right Calf			
Left Calf			
Push-ups in 60 seconds			
Pull-ups in 60 seconds/Flex Arm Hang			
Squats in 60 seconds			
Sit-ups in 60 seconds			
Sit & Reach Distance			
Heartbeat after 3 Min Stair Climb			

On average for the last 4 weeks, how much do you agree?
On a scale of 1-10 with 1 being least agreement and 10 being most agreement

		CURRENT	CHANGE
PHYSICAL HEALTH	I am clean and orderly		
	I am sleeping well		
	I am exercising well		
	I feel properly energetic		
	Total Physical Health Score:		
EMOTIONAL HEALTH	I am not feeling worried or anxious		
	I am able to relax		
	I feel a sense of tranquility		
	I am not easily annoyed or irritated		
	Total Emotional Health Score:		
INTELLECTUAL HEALTH	I am consistently learning		
	I can consider ideas that I disagree with		
	I can change my opinion when appropriate		
	I am intellectually challenged		
	Total Intellectual Health Score:		
SPIRITUAL HEALTH	I can forgive myself and others		
	I feel a strong purpose in my life		
	I accept what I cannot change		
	I practice routines to develop my spirit		
	Total Spiritual Health Score:		
SOCIAL HEALTH	I don't feel lonely		
	I enjoy spending time with others		
	I make a positive contribution to my community		
	I do not attempt to avoid people		
	Total Social Health Score:		

Total Score:		Change:	

WEEK 8 REVIEW

○ Review your 7-day goals. Did you accomplish them? **YES / NO**
If no, consider why not, and if it is still worth your time. If it is, migrate it forward into a future task.

What were the best things that happened this week?

Which activities did not work well for you this week?

What activities worked well for you this week?

Overall, this week was:

28 DAY REVIEW

○ Review your 28-day goals. Did you accomplish them? **YES / NO**
If no, consider why not, and if it is still worth your time. If it is, migrate it forward into a future task.

What were the best things that happened these last four weeks?

Which activities did not work well for you these last four weeks?

What activities worked well for you these last four weeks?

35-DAY GOAL SETTING

Review pages 42 & 43. Consider the steps you should do to achieve your quarterly goals, and what you can do to reduce the chances of the obstacles you anticipated. With those in mind, what are your goals for the next 35 days? Make them specific and achievable in 35 days.

What are some obstacles you are likely to face with these goals?

What should you do if these obstacles happen?

What can you do to prepare for or reduce the chances of them happening?

7-DAY GOAL SETTING - WEEK 9

Breakdown your 35 day goals. Consider the steps you should do to achieve the goals, and what you can do to reduce the chances of the obstacles you anticipated. With those in mind, what are your goals for the next 7 days? Make them specific and achievable in 7 days.

- **If this journal has benefitted you, order your next copy of The Focused Stoic Journal**

Why are these steps important?
- **So it will be ready for the next quarter**

What part of these steps are in your control?

424

WEEKLY THEME

Avoid Excess

WEEKLY REFLECTION

(See pg 656 for writing prompts)

35 DAY CALENDAR - WEEKS 9-13

	SUNDAY	MONDAY	TUESDAY
WEEK 9			
WEEK 10			
WEEK 11			
WEEK 12			
WEEK 13			

WEDNESDAY	THURSDAY	FRIDAY	SATURDAY

WEEK 9 PLANNER

	SUNDAY	MONDAY	TUESDAY

	WEDNESDAY	THURSDAY	FRIDAY	SATURDAY

SUNDAY — WEEK 9, DAY 1
MORNING PREPARATION

DATE:

How long did you sleep?   Meditate ☐ (pg 658)

How well did you sleep? /5   Exercise ☐

Morning Reading:

NOTES:

Review your 7-day goals. With those goals in mind, make a **'Knockout List'** of 3-5 tasks you must work to complete today. Specify the tasks, and make them something you expect you can achieve today.

What are some obstacles you are likely to face today?

What can you do to prepare for or reduce the chances of them happening?

What should you do if these obstacles happen?

In all things, deliver the maximum efficiency using the minimum effort.

(See pg 656 for writing prompts)

EVENING REVIEW

BREAKFAST	LUNCH	SUPPER	SNACKS

What were the most significant obstacles you faced today?

How could these obstacles have been worse?

How did you or how can you mitigate these obstacles?

How can you reduce the chances of them reoccurring?

How can these obstacles benefit you?

What mistakes did you make today?

What could you have done that would have been worse?

What can you do to mitigate these mistakes?

What could you do better next time?

What did you do well today?

What can you look forward to tomorrow?

Did you do what was appropriate to complete your tasks?	**YES / NO**
Did you complete your knockout list?	**YES / NO**
Are you closer to your goals today?	**YES / NO**
Did you behave according to your principles?	**YES / NO**

Fill in your Gratitude Log and 28 Day Tracking

Evening Reading:

Meditate ☐
(pg 659)

MONDAY — WEEK 9, DAY 2
MORNING PREPARATION

DATE:

How long did you sleep?   Meditate ☐   Morning Reading:
(pg 658)

How well did you sleep? /5   Exercise ☐

NOTES:

Review your 7-day goals. With those goals in mind, make a **'Knockout List'** of 3-5 tasks you must work to complete today. Specify the tasks, and make them something you expect you can achieve today.

◦ **If this journal has benefitted you, order your next copy of The Focused Stoic Journal**

What are some obstacles you are likely to face today?

What can you do to prepare for or reduce the chances of them happening?

What should you do if these obstacles happen?

"Do nothing which is of no use."

- Miyamoto Musashi

(See pg 656 for writing prompts)

EVENING REVIEW

BREAKFAST	LUNCH	SUPPER	SNACKS

What were the most significant obstacles you faced today?

How could these obstacles have been worse?

How did you or how can you mitigate these obstacles?

How can you reduce the chances of them reoccurring?

How can these obstacles benefit you?

What mistakes did you make today?

What could you have done that would have been worse?

What can you do to mitigate these mistakes?

What could you do better next time?

What did you do well today?

What can you look forward to tomorrow?

Did you do what was appropriate to complete your tasks?	**YES / NO**
Did you complete your knockout list?	**YES / NO**
Are you closer to your goals today?	**YES / NO**
Did you behave according to your principles?	**YES / NO**

Fill in your Gratitude Log and 28 Day Tracking

Evening Reading:

Meditate ☐
(pg 659)

TUESDAY — MORNING PREPARATION
WEEK 9, DAY 3

DATE:

How long did you sleep?   Meditate ☐   Morning Reading:
(pg 658)

How well did you sleep? /5   Exercise ☐

NOTES:

Review your 7-day goals. With those goals in mind, make a **'Knockout List'** of 3-5 tasks you must work to complete today. Specify the tasks, and make them something you expect you can achieve today.

What are some obstacles you are likely to face today?

What can you do to prepare for or reduce the chances of them happening?

What should you do if these obstacles happen?

> "Men's minds ought to have relaxation: they rise up better and more vigorous after rest."
>
> *- Seneca*

(See pg 656 for writing prompts)

EVENING REVIEW

BREAKFAST	LUNCH	SUPPER	SNACKS

What were the most significant obstacles you faced today?

How could these obstacles have been worse?

How did you or how can you mitigate these obstacles?

How can you reduce the chances of them reoccurring?

How can these obstacles benefit you?

What mistakes did you make today?

What could you have done that would have been worse?

What can you do to mitigate these mistakes?

What could you do better next time?

What did you do well today?

What can you look forward to tomorrow?

Did you do what was appropriate to complete your tasks?	**YES / NO**
Did you complete your knockout list?	**YES / NO**
Are you closer to your goals today?	**YES / NO**
Did you behave according to your principles?	**YES / NO**

◯ Fill in your Gratitude Log and 28 Day Tracking

Evening Reading:

Meditate ☐
(pg 659)

WEDNESDAY — WEEK 9, DAY 4
MORNING PREPARATION

DATE:

How long did you sleep?   Meditate ☐   Morning Reading:
(pg 658)

How well did you sleep? /5   Exercise ☐

NOTES:

Review your 7-day goals. With those goals in mind, make a **'Knockout List'** of 3-5 tasks you must work to complete today. Specify the tasks, and make them something you expect you can achieve today.

What are some obstacles you are likely to face today?

What can you do to prepare for or reduce the chances of them happening?

What should you do if these obstacles happen?

"Do not hold on to possessions you no longer need."

— *Miyamoto Musashi*

(See pg 656 for writing prompts)

EVENING REVIEW

BREAKFAST	LUNCH	SUPPER	SNACKS

What were the most significant obstacles you faced today?

How could these obstacles have been worse?

How did you or how can you mitigate these obstacles?

How can you reduce the chances of them reoccurring?

How can these obstacles benefit you?

What mistakes did you make today?

What could you have done that would have been worse?

What can you do to mitigate these mistakes?

What could you do better next time?

What did you do well today?

What can you look forward to tomorrow?

Did you do what was appropriate to complete your tasks?	**YES / NO**
Did you complete your knockout list?	**YES / NO**
Are you closer to your goals today?	**YES / NO**
Did you behave according to your principles?	**YES / NO**

Fill in your Gratitude Log and 28 Day Tracking

Evening Reading:

Meditate ☐
(pg 659)

THURSDAY — WEEK 9, DAY 5
MORNING PREPARATION

DATE:

How long did you sleep? Meditate ☐   Morning Reading:
(pg 658)

How well did you sleep? /5   Exercise ☐

NOTES:

Review your 7-day goals. With those goals in mind, make a **'Knockout List'** of 3-5 tasks you must work to complete today. Specify the tasks, and make them something you expect you can achieve today.

What are some obstacles you are likely to face today?

What can you do to prepare for or reduce the chances of them happening?

What should you do if these obstacles happen?

> "Make yourself neither a tyrant nor a slave to any person"
>
> - *Marcus Aurelius*

(See pg 656 for writing prompts)

EVENING REVIEW

BREAKFAST	LUNCH	SUPPER	SNACKS

What were the most significant obstacles you faced today?

How could these obstacles have been worse?

How did you or how can you mitigate these obstacles?

How can you reduce the chances of them reoccurring?

How can these obstacles benefit you?

What mistakes did you make today?

What could you have done that would have been worse?

What can you do to mitigate these mistakes?

What could you do better next time?

What did you do well today?

What can you look forward to tomorrow?

Did you do what was appropriate to complete your tasks?	YES / NO
Did you complete your knockout list?	YES / NO
Are you closer to your goals today?	YES / NO
Did you behave according to your principles?	YES / NO

◯ Fill in your Gratitude Log and 28 Day Tracking	Evening Reading:

Meditate ☐
(pg 659)

FRIDAY — MORNING PREPARATION
WEEK 9, DAY 6

DATE:

How long did you sleep?   Meditate ☐ (pg 658)

How well did you sleep? /5   Exercise ☐

Morning Reading:

NOTES:

Review your 7-day goals. With those goals in mind, make a **'Knockout List'** of 3-5 tasks you must work to complete today. Specify the tasks, and make them something you expect you can achieve today.

What are some obstacles you are likely to face today?

What can you do to prepare for or reduce the chances of them happening?

What should you do if these obstacles happen?

> "How much more harmful are the consequences of anger and grief than the circumstances that aroused them in us!"
> — *Marcus Aurelius*

(See pg 656 for writing prompts)

EVENING REVIEW

BREAKFAST	LUNCH	SUPPER	SNACKS

What were the most significant obstacles you faced today?

How could these obstacles have been worse?

How did you or how can you mitigate these obstacles?

How can you reduce the chances of them reoccurring?

How can these obstacles benefit you?

What mistakes did you make today?

What could you have done that would have been worse?

What can you do to mitigate these mistakes?

What could you do better next time?

What did you do well today?

What can you look forward to tomorrow?

Did you do what was appropriate to complete your tasks?	**YES / NO**
Did you complete your knockout list?	**YES / NO**
Are you closer to your goals today?	**YES / NO**
Did you behave according to your principles?	**YES / NO**

Fill in your Gratitude Log and 28 Day Tracking

Evening Reading:

Meditate ☐
(pg 659)

SATURDAY — WEEK 9, DAY 7
MORNING PREPARATION

DATE:

How long did you sleep? Meditate ☐   Morning Reading:
(pg 658)

How well did you sleep? /5   Exercise ☐

NOTES:

Review your 7-day goals. With those goals in mind, make a **'Knockout List'** of 3-5 tasks you must work to complete today. Specify the tasks, and make them something you expect you can achieve today.

What are some obstacles you are likely to face today?

What can you do to prepare for or reduce the chances of them happening?

What should you do if these obstacles happen?

> "But all examples of excess become a fault."
>
> *- Seneca*

(See pg 656 for writing prompts)

EVENING REVIEW

BREAKFAST	LUNCH	SUPPER	SNACKS

What were the most significant obstacles you faced today?

How could these obstacles have been worse?

How did you or how can you mitigate these obstacles?

How can you reduce the chances of them reoccurring?

How can these obstacles benefit you?

What mistakes did you make today?

What could you have done that would have been worse?

What can you do to mitigate these mistakes?

What could you do better next time?

What did you do well today?

What can you look forward to tomorrow?

Did you do what was appropriate to complete your tasks?	**YES / NO**
Did you complete your knockout list?	**YES / NO**
Are you closer to your goals today?	**YES / NO**
Did you behave according to your principles?	**YES / NO**

Fill in your Gratitude Log and 28 Day Tracking

Evening Reading:

Meditate ☐
(pg 659)

WEEK 9 GRATITUDE LOG

Write briefly about anything that you have to be grateful for for each day.

If you are having difficulty thinking about what to write, you can consult the prompts on page 657.

SUNDAY

MONDAY

TUESDAY

WEDNESDAY

THURSDAY

FRIDAY

SATURDAY

WEEKLY PREMEDITATION OF OBSTACLES

Think of a significant obstacle happening to you, or think about suffering a significant loss. Imagine it as if it were happening now. Describe it in detail.

What would be the best way to react to this happening?

What are some things you now enjoy which you could no longer enjoy if this happens to you? Describe what you enjoy about it in detail.

How could you repair any damage caused if this happened?

What could you still enjoy in your life if this happened?

What could you do to prepare for or reduce the chances of this happening?

It's a possibility that this could happen to you. But it hasn't yet. What can you do to appreciate what you have now?

WEEK 9 REVIEW

○ Review your 7-day goals. Did you accomplish them? **YES / NO**
If no, consider why not, and if it is still worth your time. If it is, migrate it forward into a future task.

What were the best things that happened this week?

Which activities did not work well for you this week?

What activities worked well for you this week?

Overall, this week was:

7-DAY GOAL SETTING - WEEK 10

Review your 35 day goals. Consider the steps you should do to achieve the goals, and what you can do to reduce the chances of the obstacles you anticipated. With those in mind, what are your goals for the next 7 days? Make them specific and achievable in 7 days.

Why are these steps important?

What part of these steps are in your control?

WEEKLY THEME

Make the World Better

WEEKLY REFLECTION

(See pg 656 for writing prompts)

474

WEEK 10 PLANNER

	SUNDAY	MONDAY	TUESDAY

	WEDNESDAY	THURSDAY	FRIDAY	SATURDAY

SUNDAY
MORNING PREPARATION
WEEK 10, DAY 1

DATE:

How long did you sleep?   Meditate ☐   Morning Reading:
(pg 658)

How well did you sleep? /5   Exercise ☐

NOTES:

Review your 7-day goals. With those goals in mind, make a **'Knockout List'** of 3-5 tasks you must work to complete today. Specify the tasks, and make them something you expect you can achieve today.

What are some obstacles you are likely to face today?

What can you do to prepare for or reduce the chances of them happening?

What should you do if these obstacles happen?

> "Associate with people who are likely to improve you. Welcome those who you are capable of improving. The process is a mutual one: men learn as they teach."
>
> *- Seneca*

(See pg 656 for writing prompts)

EVENING REVIEW

BREAKFAST	LUNCH	SUPPER	SNACKS

What were the most significant obstacles you faced today?

How could these obstacles have been worse?

How did you or how can you mitigate these obstacles?

How can you reduce the chances of them reoccurring?

How can these obstacles benefit you?

What mistakes did you make today?

What could you have done that would have been worse?

What can you do to mitigate these mistakes?

What could you do better next time?

What did you do well today?

What can you look forward to tomorrow?

Did you do what was appropriate to complete your tasks?	**YES / NO**
Did you complete your knockout list?	**YES / NO**
Are you closer to your goals today?	**YES / NO**
Did you behave according to your principles?	**YES / NO**

Fill in your Gratitude Log and 28 Day Tracking

Evening Reading:

Meditate ☐
(pg 659)

MONDAY — MORNING PREPARATION
WEEK 10, DAY 2

DATE:

How long did you sleep? Meditate ☐ (pg 658)

How well did you sleep? /5 Exercise ☐

Morning Reading:

NOTES:

Review your 7-day goals. With those goals in mind, make a **'Knockout List'** of 3-5 tasks you must work to complete today. Specify the tasks, and make them something you expect you can achieve today.

What are some obstacles you are likely to face today?

What can you do to prepare for or reduce the chances of them happening?

What should you do if these obstacles happen?

> "The ultimate test of a moral society is the kind of world that it leaves to its children."
>
> *- Dietrich Bonhoffer*

(See pg 656 for writing prompts)

EVENING REVIEW

BREAKFAST	LUNCH	SUPPER	SNACKS

What were the most significant obstacles you faced today?

How could these obstacles have been worse?

How did you or how can you mitigate these obstacles?

How can you reduce the chances of them reoccurring?

How can these obstacles benefit you?

What mistakes did you make today?

What could you have done that would have been worse?

What can you do to mitigate these mistakes?

What could you do better next time?

What did you do well today?

What can you look forward to tomorrow?

Did you do what was appropriate to complete your tasks?	**YES / NO**
Did you complete your knockout list?	**YES / NO**
Are you closer to your goals today?	**YES / NO**
Did you behave according to your principles?	**YES / NO**

Fill in your Gratitude Log and 28 Day Tracking

Evening Reading:

Meditate ☐
(pg 659)

TUESDAY — MORNING PREPARATION
WEEK 10, DAY 3

DATE:

How long did you sleep?   Meditate ☐ (pg 658)

How well did you sleep? /5   Exercise ☐

Morning Reading:

NOTES:

Review your 7-day goals. With those goals in mind, make a **'Knockout List'** of 3-5 tasks you must work to complete today. Specify the tasks, and make them something you expect you can achieve today.

What are some obstacles you are likely to face today?

What can you do to prepare for or reduce the chances of them happening?

What should you do if these obstacles happen?

> "If you want any good, get it from within."
>
> *- Epictetus*

(See pg 656 for writing prompts)

EVENING REVIEW

BREAKFAST	LUNCH	SUPPER	SNACKS

What were the most significant obstacles you faced today?

How could these obstacles have been worse?

How did you or how can you mitigate these obstacles?

How can you reduce the chances of them reoccurring?

How can these obstacles benefit you?

What mistakes did you make today?

What could you have done that would have been worse?

What can you do to mitigate these mistakes?

What could you do better next time?

What did you do well today?

What can you look forward to tomorrow?

Did you do what was appropriate to complete your tasks?	**YES / NO**
Did you complete your knockout list?	**YES / NO**
Are you closer to your goals today?	**YES / NO**
Did you behave according to your principles?	**YES / NO**

Fill in your Gratitude Log and 28 Day Tracking

Evening Reading:

Meditate ☐
(pg 659)

WEDNESDAY — WEEK 10, DAY 4
MORNING PREPARATION

DATE:

How long did you sleep? Meditate ☐   Morning Reading:
                         (pg 658)
How well did you sleep? /5   Exercise ☐

NOTES:

Review your 7-day goals. With those goals in mind, make a **'Knockout List'** of 3-5 tasks you must work to complete today. Specify the tasks, and make them something you expect you can achieve today.

What are some obstacles you are likely to face today?

What can you do to prepare for or reduce the chances of them happening?

What should you do if these obstacles happen?

All things tend towards entropy: including health, wealth, virtue, and freedom. Tend to them or watch them dissappear.

(See pg 656 for writing prompts)

EVENING REVIEW

BREAKFAST	LUNCH	SUPPER	SNACKS

What were the most significant obstacles you faced today?

How could these obstacles have been worse?

How did you or how can you mitigate these obstacles?

How can you reduce the chances of them reoccurring?

How can these obstacles benefit you?

What mistakes did you make today?

What could you have done that would have been worse?

What can you do to mitigate these mistakes?

What could you do better next time?

What did you do well today?

What can you look forward to tomorrow?

Did you do what was appropriate to complete your tasks?	**YES / NO**
Did you complete your knockout list?	**YES / NO**
Are you closer to your goals today?	**YES / NO**
Did you behave according to your principles?	**YES / NO**

◯ Fill in your Gratitude Log and 28 Day Tracking

Evening Reading:

Meditate ☐
(pg 659)

THURSDAY — WEEK 10, DAY 5
MORNING PREPARATION

DATE:

How long did you sleep? Meditate ☐ Morning Reading:
(pg 658)

How well did you sleep? /5 Exercise ☐

NOTES:

Review your 7-day goals. With those goals in mind, make a **'Knockout List'** of 3-5 tasks you must work to complete today. Specify the tasks, and make them something you expect you can achieve today.

What are some obstacles you are likely to face today?

What can you do to prepare for or reduce the chances of them happening?

What should you do if these obstacles happen?

Be prepared.

(See pg 656 for writing prompts)

EVENING REVIEW

BREAKFAST	LUNCH	SUPPER	SNACKS

What were the most significant obstacles you faced today?

How could these obstacles have been worse?

How did you or how can you mitigate these obstacles?

How can you reduce the chances of them reoccurring?

How can these obstacles benefit you?

What mistakes did you make today?

What could you have done that would have been worse?

What can you do to mitigate these mistakes?

What could you do better next time?

What did you do well today?

What can you look forward to tomorrow?

Did you do what was appropriate to complete your tasks?	**YES / NO**
Did you complete your knockout list?	**YES / NO**
Are you closer to your goals today?	**YES / NO**
Did you behave according to your principles?	**YES / NO**

◯ Fill in your Gratitude Log and 28 Day Tracking

Evening Reading:

Meditate ☐
(pg 659)

FRIDAY
MORNING PREPARATION
WEEK 10, DAY 6

DATE:

How long did you sleep?   Meditate ☐   Morning Reading:
(pg 658)

How well did you sleep? /5   Exercise ☐

NOTES:

Review your 7-day goals. With those goals in mind, make a **'Knockout List'** of 3-5 tasks you must work to complete today. Specify the tasks, and make them something you expect you can achieve today.

What are some obstacles you are likely to face today?

What can you do to prepare for or reduce the chances of them happening?

What should you do if these obstacles happen?

> "A man's true delight is to do the things he was made for."
>
> *- Marcus Aurelius*

(See pg 656 for writing prompts)

EVENTING REVIEW

BREAKFAST	LUNCH	SUPPER	SNACKS

What were the most significant obstacles you faced today?

How could these obstacles have been worse?

How did you or how can you mitigate these obstacles?

How can you reduce the chances of them reoccurring?

How can these obstacles benefit you?

What mistakes did you make today?

What could you have done that would have been worse?

What can you do to mitigate these mistakes?

What could you do better next time?

What did you do well today?

What can you look forward to tomorrow?

Did you do what was appropriate to complete your tasks?	**YES / NO**
Did you complete your knockout list?	**YES / NO**
Are you closer to your goals today?	**YES / NO**
Did you behave according to your principles?	**YES / NO**

Fill in your Gratitude Log and 28 Day Tracking

Evening Reading:

Meditate ☐
(pg 659)

SATURDAY — MORNING PREPARATION
WEEK 10, DAY 7

DATE:

How long did you sleep? Meditate ☐   Morning Reading:
(pg 658)

How well did you sleep? /5 Exercise ☐

NOTES:

Review your 7-day goals. With those goals in mind, make a **'Knockout List'** of 3-5 tasks you must work to complete today. Specify the tasks, and make them something you expect you can achieve today.

What are some obstacles you are likely to face today?

What can you do to prepare for or reduce the chances of them happening?

What should you do if these obstacles happen?

"I am convinced that people are much better off when their whole city is flourishing than when certain citizens prosper but the community has gone off course. When a man is doing well for himself but his country is falling to pieces he goes to pieces along with it, but a struggling individual has much better hopes if his country is thriving."

- Marcus Aurelius

(See pg 656 for writing prompts)

EVENING REVIEW

BREAKFAST	LUNCH	SUPPER	SNACKS

What were the most significant obstacles you faced today?

How could these obstacles have been worse?

How did you or how can you mitigate these obstacles?

How can you reduce the chances of them reoccurring?

How can these obstacles benefit you?

What mistakes did you make today?

What could you have done that would have been worse?

What can you do to mitigate these mistakes?

What could you do better next time?

What did you do well today?

What can you look forward to tomorrow?

Did you do what was appropriate to complete your tasks?	**YES / NO**
Did you complete your knockout list?	**YES / NO**
Are you closer to your goals today?	**YES / NO**
Did you behave according to your principles?	**YES / NO**

Fill in your Gratitude Log and 28 Day Tracking

Evening Reading:

Meditate ☐
(pg 659)

WEEK 10 GRATITUDE LOG

Write briefly about anything that you have to be grateful for for each day.

If you are having difficulty thinking about what to write, you can consult the prompts on page 657.

SUNDAY

MONDAY

TUESDAY

WEDNESDAY

THURSDAY

FRIDAY

SATURDAY

WEEKLY PREMEDITATION OF OBSTACLES

Think of a significant obstacle happening to you, or think about suffering a significant loss. Imagine it as if it were happening now. Describe it in detail.

What would be the best way to react to this happening?

What are some things you now enjoy which you could no longer enjoy if this happens to you? Describe what you enjoy about it in detail.

How could you repair any damage caused if this happened?

What could you still enjoy in your life if this happened?

What could you do to prepare for or reduce the chances of this happening?

It's a possibility that this could happen to you. But it hasn't yet. What can you do to appreciate what you have now?

WEEK 10 REVIEW

Review your 7-day goals. Did you accomplish them? **YES / NO**
If no, consider why not, and if it is still worth your time. If it is, migrate it forward into a future task.

What were the best things that happened this week?

Which activities did not work well for you this week?

What activities worked well for you this week?

Overall, this week was:

7-DAY GOAL SETTING - WEEK 11

Review your 35 day goals. Consider the steps you should do to achieve the goals, and what you can do to reduce the chances of the obstacles you anticipated. With those in mind, what are your goals for the next 7 days? Make them specific and achievable in 7 days.

Why are these steps important?

What part of these steps are in your control?

WEEKLY THEME

Seek Order, Fairness, and Justice

WEEKLY REFLECTION

(See pg 656 for writing prompts)

519

WEEK 11 PLANNER

	SUNDAY	MONDAY	TUESDAY

	WEDNESDAY	THURSDAY	FRIDAY	SATURDAY

SUNDAY — MORNING PREPARATION
WEEK 11, DAY 1

DATE:

How long did you sleep? Meditate ☐
(pg 658)

How well did you sleep? /5 Exercise ☐

Morning Reading:

NOTES:

Review your 7-day goals. With those goals in mind, make a **'Knockout List'** of 3-5 tasks you must work to complete today. Specify the tasks, and make them something you expect you can achieve today.

What are some obstacles you are likely to face today?

What can you do to prepare for or reduce the chances of them happening?

What should you do if these obstacles happen?

> "Until you have reasonable evidence to the contrary, assume the best interpretation of a person's arguments, actions, and intentions."

(See pg 656 for writing prompts)

EVENING REVIEW

BREAKFAST	LUNCH	SUPPER	SNACKS

What were the most significant obstacles you faced today?

How could these obstacles have been worse?

How did you or how can you mitigate these obstacles?

How can you reduce the chances of them reoccurring?

How can these obstacles benefit you?

What mistakes did you make today?

What could you have done that would have been worse?

What can you do to mitigate these mistakes?

What could you do better next time?

What did you do well today?

What can you look forward to tomorrow?

Did you do what was appropriate to complete your tasks?	YES / NO
Did you complete your knockout list?	YES / NO
Are you closer to your goals today?	YES / NO
Did you behave according to your principles?	YES / NO

○ Fill in your Gratitude Log and 28 Day Tracking

Evening Reading:

Meditate ☐
(pg 659)

MONDAY — MORNING PREPARATION
WEEK 11, DAY 2

DATE:

How long did you sleep?   Meditate ☐   Morning Reading:
(pg 658)

How well did you sleep? /5   Exercise ☐

NOTES:

Review your 7-day goals. With those goals in mind, make a **'Knockout List'** of 3-5 tasks you must work to complete today. Specify the tasks, and make them something you expect you can achieve today.

What are some obstacles you are likely to face today?

What can you do to prepare for or reduce the chances of them happening?

What should you do if these obstacles happen?

> "There is but one thing of real value - to cultivate truth and justice, and to live without anger in the midst of lying and unjust men."
>
> *- Marcus Aurelius*

(See pg 656 for writing prompts)

EVENING REVIEW

BREAKFAST	LUNCH	SUPPER	SNACKS

What were the most significant obstacles you faced today?

How could these obstacles have been worse?

How did you or how can you mitigate these obstacles?

How can you reduce the chances of them reoccurring?

How can these obstacles benefit you?

What mistakes did you make today?

What could you have done that would have been worse?

What can you do to mitigate these mistakes?

What could you do better next time?

What did you do well today?

What can you look forward to tomorrow?

Did you do what was appropriate to complete your tasks?	**YES / NO**
Did you complete your knockout list?	**YES / NO**
Are you closer to your goals today?	**YES / NO**
Did you behave according to your principles?	**YES / NO**

Fill in your Gratitude Log and 28 Day Tracking

Evening Reading:

Meditate ☐
(pg 659)

TUESDAY — WEEK 11, DAY 3
MORNING PREPARATION

DATE:

How long did you sleep?   Meditate ☐   Morning Reading:
                                (pg 658)

How well did you sleep? /5   Exercise ☐

NOTES:

Review your 7-day goals. With those goals in mind, make a **'Knockout List'** of 3-5 tasks you must work to complete today. Specify the tasks, and make them something you expect you can achieve today.

What are some obstacles you are likely to face today?

What can you do to prepare for or reduce the chances of them happening?

What should you do if these obstacles happen?

"The wise man will not pardon any crime that ought to be punished, but he will accomplish, in a nobler way, all that is sought in pardoning. He will spare some and watch over some, because of their youth, and others on account of their ignorance. His clemency will not fall short of justice, but will fulfill it perfectly."

- *Seneca*

(See pg 656 for writing prompts)

EVENING REVIEW

BREAKFAST	LUNCH	SUPPER	SNACKS

What were the most significant obstacles you faced today?

How could these obstacles have been worse?

How did you or how can you mitigate these obstacles?

How can you reduce the chances of them reoccurring?

How can these obstacles benefit you?

What mistakes did you make today?

What could you have done that would have been worse?

What can you do to mitigate these mistakes?

What could you do better next time?

What did you do well today?

What can you look forward to tomorrow?

Did you do what was appropriate to complete your tasks?	YES / NO
Did you complete your knockout list?	YES / NO
Are you closer to your goals today?	YES / NO
Did you behave according to your principles?	YES / NO

Fill in your Gratitude Log and 28 Day Tracking

Evening Reading:

Meditate ☐
(pg 659)

WEDNESDAY — WEEK 11, DAY 4
MORNING PREPARATION

DATE:

How long did you sleep?　　　Meditate ☐　　　Morning Reading:
(pg 658)

How well did you sleep?　/5　Exercise ☐

NOTES:

Review your 7-day goals. With those goals in mind, make a **'Knockout List'** of 3-5 tasks you must work to complete today. Specify the tasks, and make them something you expect you can achieve today.

What are some obstacles you are likely to face today?

What can you do to prepare for or reduce the chances of them happening?

What should you do if these obstacles happen?

> "And yet life, Lucilius, is really a battle."
>
> *- Seneca*

(See pg 656 for writing prompts)

EVENING REVIEW

BREAKFAST	LUNCH	SUPPER	SNACKS

What were the most significant obstacles you faced today?

How could these obstacles have been worse?

How did you or how can you mitigate these obstacles?

How can you reduce the chances of them reoccurring?

How can these obstacles benefit you?

What mistakes did you make today?

What could you have done that would have been worse?

What can you do to mitigate these mistakes?

What could you do better next time?

What did you do well today?

What can you look forward to tomorrow?

Did you do what was appropriate to complete your tasks?	**YES / NO**
Did you complete your knockout list?	**YES / NO**
Are you closer to your goals today?	**YES / NO**
Did you behave according to your principles?	**YES / NO**

Fill in your Gratitude Log and 28 Day Tracking

Evening Reading:

Meditate ☐
(pg 659)

THURSDAY
MORNING PREPARATION
WEEK 11, DAY 5

DATE:

How long did you sleep?   Meditate ☐   Morning Reading:
(pg 658)

How well did you sleep? /5   Exercise ☐

NOTES:

Review your 7-day goals. With those goals in mind, make a **'Knockout List'** of 3-5 tasks you must work to complete today. Specify the tasks, and make them something you expect you can achieve today.

What are some obstacles you are likely to face today?

What can you do to prepare for or reduce the chances of them happening?

What should you do if these obstacles happen?

> "The task of art today is to bring chaos into order."
>
> *- Theodor Adorno*

(See pg 656 for writing prompts)

EVENING REVIEW

BREAKFAST	LUNCH	SUPPER	SNACKS

What were the most significant obstacles you faced today?

How could these obstacles have been worse?

How did you or how can you mitigate these obstacles?

How can you reduce the chances of them reoccurring?

How can these obstacles benefit you?

What mistakes did you make today?

What could you have done that would have been worse?

What can you do to mitigate these mistakes?

What could you do better next time?

What did you do well today?

What can you look forward to tomorrow?

Did you do what was appropriate to complete your tasks?	**YES / NO**
Did you complete your knockout list?	**YES / NO**
Are you closer to your goals today?	**YES / NO**
Did you behave according to your principles?	**YES / NO**

Fill in your Gratitude Log and 28 Day Tracking

Evening Reading:

Meditate ☐
(pg 659)

FRIDAY — WEEK 11, DAY 6
MORNING PREPARATION

DATE:

How long did you sleep? Meditate ☐
(pg 658)

How well did you sleep? /5 Exercise ☐

Morning Reading:

NOTES:

Review your 7-day goals. With those goals in mind, make a **'Knockout List'** of 3-5 tasks you must work to complete today. Specify the tasks, and make them something you expect you can achieve today.

What are some obstacles you are likely to face today?

What can you do to prepare for or reduce the chances of them happening?

What should you do if these obstacles happen?

> "For to scheme how to bite back the biter and to return evil for evil is the act not of a human being but of a wild beast, which is incapable of reasoning that the majority of wrongs are done to men through ignorance and misunderstanding, from which man will cease as soon as he has been taught"
>
> — *Musonius Rufus*

(See pg 656 for writing prompts)

EVENING REVIEW

BREAKFAST	LUNCH	SUPPER	SNACKS

What were the most significant obstacles you faced today?

How could these obstacles have been worse?

How did you or how can you mitigate these obstacles?

How can you reduce the chances of them reoccurring?

How can these obstacles benefit you?

What mistakes did you make today?

What could you have done that would have been worse?

What can you do to mitigate these mistakes?

What could you do better next time?

What did you do well today?

What can you look forward to tomorrow?

Did you do what was appropriate to complete your tasks?	YES / NO
Did you complete your knockout list?	YES / NO
Are you closer to your goals today?	YES / NO
Did you behave according to your principles?	YES / NO

Fill in your Gratitude Log and 28 Day Tracking

Evening Reading:

Meditate ☐
(pg 659)

SATURDAY
MORNING PREPARATION
WEEK 11, DAY 7

DATE:

How long did you sleep?   Meditate ☐   Morning Reading:
(pg 658)

How well did you sleep? /5   Exercise ☐

NOTES:

Review your 7-day goals. With those goals in mind, make a **'Knockout List'** of 3-5 tasks you must work to complete today. Specify the tasks, and make them something you expect you can achieve today.

What are some obstacles you are likely to face today?

What can you do to prepare for or reduce the chances of them happening?

What should you do if these obstacles happen?

> "Let the punishment be equal with the offence... Care should be taken that the punishment does not exceed the guilt; and also that some men do not suffer for offenses for which others are not even indicted."
>
> *- Cicero*

(See pg 656 for writing prompts)

EVENING REVIEW

BREAKFAST	LUNCH	SUPPER	SNACKS

What were the most significant obstacles you faced today?

How could these obstacles have been worse?

How did you or how can you mitigate these obstacles?

How can you reduce the chances of them reoccurring?

How can these obstacles benefit you?

What mistakes did you make today?

What could you have done that would have been worse?

What can you do to mitigate these mistakes?

What could you do better next time?

What did you do well today?

What can you look forward to tomorrow?

Did you do what was appropriate to complete your tasks?	YES / NO
Did you complete your knockout list?	YES / NO
Are you closer to your goals today?	YES / NO
Did you behave according to your principles?	YES / NO

Fill in your Gratitude Log and 28 Day Tracking

Evening Reading:

Meditate ☐
(pg 659)

551

WEEK 11 GRATITUDE LOG

Write briefly about anything that you have to be grateful for for each day.

If you are having difficulty thinking about what to write, you can consult the prompts on page 657.

SUNDAY

MONDAY

TUESDAY

WEDNESDAY

THURSDAY

FRIDAY

SATURDAY

WEEKLY PREMEDITATION OF OBSTACLES

Think of a significant obstacle happening to you, or think about suffering a significant loss. Imagine it as if it were happening now. Describe it in detail.

What would be the best way to react to this happening?

What are some things you now enjoy which you could no longer enjoy if this happens to you? Describe what you enjoy about it in detail.

How could you repair any damage caused if this happened?

What could you still enjoy in your life if this happened?

What could you do to prepare for or reduce the chances of this happening?

It's a possibility that this could happen to you. But it hasn't yet. What can you do to appreciate what you have now?

WEEK 11 REVIEW

○ Review your 7-day goals. Did you accomplish them? **YES / NO**
If no, consider why not, and if it is still worth your time. If it is, migrate it forward into a future task.

What were the best things that happened this week?

Which activities did not work well for you this week?

What activities worked well for you this week?

Overall, this week was:

7-DAY GOAL SETTING - WEEK 12

Review your 35 day goals. Consider the steps you should do to achieve the goals, and what you can do to reduce the chances of the obstacles you anticipated. With those in mind, what are your goals for the next 7 days? Make them specific and achievable in 7 days.

Why are these steps important?

What part of these steps are in your control?

WEEKLY THEME

Hate Nothing, But Be Courageous

WEEKLY REFLECTION

(See pg 656 for writing prompts)

WEEK 12 PLANNER

	SUNDAY	MONDAY	TUESDAY

	WEDNESDAY	THURSDAY	FRIDAY	SATURDAY

SUNDAY — WEEK 12, DAY 1
MORNING PREPARATION

DATE:

How long did you sleep?   Meteorite ☐   Meditate ☐ (pg 658)

How well did you sleep? /5   Exercise ☐

Morning Reading:

NOTES:

Review your 7-day goals. With those goals in mind, make a **'Knockout List'** of 3-5 tasks you must work to complete today. Specify the tasks, and make them something you expect you can achieve today.

What are some obstacles you are likely to face today?

What can you do to prepare for or reduce the chances of them happening?

What should you do if these obstacles happen?

> "Never let the future disturb you. You will meet it, if you have to, with the same weapons of reason which today arm you against the present."
>
> *- Marcus Aurelius*

(See pg 656 for writing prompts)

EVENING REVIEW

BREAKFAST	LUNCH	SUPPER	SNACKS

What were the most significant obstacles you faced today?

How could these obstacles have been worse?

How did you or how can you mitigate these obstacles?

How can you reduce the chances of them reoccurring?

How can these obstacles benefit you?

What mistakes did you make today?

What could you have done that would have been worse?

What can you do to mitigate these mistakes?

What could you do better next time?

What did you do well today?

What can you look forward to tomorrow?

Did you do what was appropriate to complete your tasks?	**YES / NO**
Did you complete your knockout list?	**YES / NO**
Are you closer to your goals today?	**YES / NO**
Did you behave according to your principles?	**YES / NO**

Fill in your Gratitude Log and 28 Day Tracking

Evening Reading:

Meditate ☐
(pg 659)

MONDAY — MORNING PREPARATION
WEEK 12, DAY 2

DATE:

How long did you sleep? Meditate ☐ Morning Reading:
(pg 658)
How well did you sleep? /5 Exercise ☐

NOTES:

Review your 7-day goals. With those goals in mind, make a **'Knockout List'** of 3-5 tasks you must work to complete today. Specify the tasks, and make them something you expect you can achieve today.

What are some obstacles you are likely to face today?

What can you do to prepare for or reduce the chances of them happening?

What should you do if these obstacles happen?

> "It is shameful to hate a person who deserves your praises; but how much more shameful it is to hate someone for the very cause that makes him deserve your pity."
>
> *- Seneca*

(See pg 656 for writing prompts)

EVENING REVIEW

BREAKFAST	LUNCH	SUPPER	SNACKS

What were the most significant obstacles you faced today?

How could these obstacles have been worse?

How did you or how can you mitigate these obstacles?

How can you reduce the chances of them reoccurring?

How can these obstacles benefit you?

What mistakes did you make today?

What could you have done that would have been worse?

What can you do to mitigate these mistakes?

What could you do better next time?

What did you do well today?

What can you look forward to tomorrow?

Did you do what was appropriate to complete your tasks?	**YES / NO**
Did you complete your knockout list?	**YES / NO**
Are you closer to your goals today?	**YES / NO**
Did you behave according to your principles?	**YES / NO**

Fill in your Gratitude Log and 28 Day Tracking

Evening Reading:

Meditate ☐
(pg 659)

TUESDAY — WEEK 12, DAY 3
MORNING PREPARATION

DATE:

How long did you sleep?   Meditate ☐
(pg 658)

How well did you sleep? /5   Exercise ☐

Morning Reading:

NOTES:

Review your 7-day goals. With those goals in mind, make a **'Knockout List'** of 3-5 tasks you must work to complete today. Specify the tasks, and make them something you expect you can achieve today.

What are some obstacles you are likely to face today?

What can you do to prepare for or reduce the chances of them happening?

What should you do if these obstacles happen?

"Silence in the face of evil is itself evil. Not to speak against evil is to speak out for it. Not to act against evil is to act for it."

- Dietrich Bonhoffer

(See pg 656 for writing prompts)

EVENING REVIEW

BREAKFAST	LUNCH	SUPPER	SNACKS

What were the most significant obstacles you faced today?

How could these obstacles have been worse?

How did you or how can you mitigate these obstacles?

How can you reduce the chances of them reoccurring?

How can these obstacles benefit you?

What mistakes did you make today?

What could you have done that would have been worse?

What can you do to mitigate these mistakes?

What could you do better next time?

What did you do well today?

What can you look forward to tomorrow?

Did you do what was appropriate to complete your tasks?	**YES / NO**
Did you complete your knockout list?	**YES / NO**
Are you closer to your goals today?	**YES / NO**
Did you behave according to your principles?	**YES / NO**

Fill in your Gratitude Log and 28 Day Tracking

Evening Reading:

Meditate ☐
(pg 659)

WEDNESDAY — WEEK 12, DAY 4
MORNING PREPARATION

DATE:

How long did you sleep? Meditate ☐ (pg 658)

How well did you sleep? /5 Exercise ☐

Morning Reading:

NOTES:

Review your 7-day goals. With those goals in mind, make a **'Knockout List'** of 3-5 tasks you must work to complete today. Specify the tasks, and make them something you expect you can achieve today.

What are some obstacles you are likely to face today?

What can you do to prepare for or reduce the chances of them happening?

What should you do if these obstacles happen?

> "In each of us, two natures are at war – the good and the evil. All our lives the fight goes on between them, and one of them must conquer. But in our own hands lies the power to choose – what we want most to be we are."
>
> *- Robert Louis Stevenson*

(See pg 656 for writing prompts)

EVENING REVIEW

BREAKFAST	LUNCH	SUPPER	SNACKS

What were the most significant obstacles you faced today?

How could these obstacles have been worse?

How did you or how can you mitigate these obstacles?

How can you reduce the chances of them reoccurring?

How can these obstacles benefit you?

What mistakes did you make today?

What could you have done that would have been worse?

What can you do to mitigate these mistakes?

What could you do better next time?

What did you do well today?

What can you look forward to tomorrow?

Did you do what was appropriate to complete your tasks?	**YES / NO**
Did you complete your knockout list?	**YES / NO**
Are you closer to your goals today?	**YES / NO**
Did you behave according to your principles?	**YES / NO**

Fill in your Gratitude Log and 28 Day Tracking

Evening Reading:

Meditate ☐
(pg 659)

THURSDAY
MORNING PREPARATION
WEEK 12, DAY 5

DATE:

How long did you sleep?   Meditate ☐ (pg 658)

How well did you sleep? /5   Exercise ☐

Morning Reading:

NOTES:

Review your 7-day goals. With those goals in mind, make a **'Knockout List'** of 3-5 tasks you must work to complete today. Specify the tasks, and make them something you expect you can achieve today.

What are some obstacles you are likely to face today?

What can you do to prepare for or reduce the chances of them happening?

What should you do if these obstacles happen?

"The sword is the mind. When the mind is right, the sword it right. When the mind is not right, the sword is also not right. He who wishes to study the way of the sword must first study his mind."

- Toranosuke Shimada

(See pg 656 for writing prompts)

EVENING REVIEW

BREAKFAST	LUNCH	SUPPER	SNACKS

What were the most significant obstacles you faced today?

How could these obstacles have been worse?

How did you or how can you mitigate these obstacles?

How can you reduce the chances of them reoccurring?

How can these obstacles benefit you?

What mistakes did you make today?

What could you have done that would have been worse?

What can you do to mitigate these mistakes?

What could you do better next time?

What did you do well today?

What can you look forward to tomorrow?

Did you do what was appropriate to complete your tasks?	**YES / NO**
Did you complete your knockout list?	**YES / NO**
Are you closer to your goals today?	**YES / NO**
Did you behave according to your principles?	**YES / NO**

Fill in your Gratitude Log and 28 Day Tracking

Evening Reading:

Meditate ☐
(pg 659)

FRIDAY — MORNING PREPARATION
WEEK 12, DAY 6

DATE:

How long did you sleep?   Meditate ☐   Morning Reading:
(pg 658)

How well did you sleep? /5   Exercise ☐

NOTES:

Review your 7-day goals. With those goals in mind, make a **'Knockout List'** of 3-5 tasks you must work to complete today. Specify the tasks, and make them something you expect you can achieve today.

What are some obstacles you are likely to face today?

What can you do to prepare for or reduce the chances of them happening?

What should you do if these obstacles happen?

"The one uses his troops to safeguard the piece of his kingdom. The other uses them to quell great hatred by great terror."

- Seneca

(See pg 656 for writing prompts)

EVENING REVIEW

BREAKFAST	LUNCH	SUPPER	SNACKS

What were the most significant obstacles you faced today?

How could these obstacles have been worse?

How did you or how can you mitigate these obstacles?

How can you reduce the chances of them reoccurring?

How can these obstacles benefit you?

What mistakes did you make today?

What could you have done that would have been worse?

What can you do to mitigate these mistakes?

What could you do better next time?

What did you do well today?

What can you look forward to tomorrow?

Did you do what was appropriate to complete your tasks?	**YES / NO**
Did you complete your knockout list?	**YES / NO**
Are you closer to your goals today?	**YES / NO**
Did you behave according to your principles?	**YES / NO**

Fill in your Gratitude Log and 28 Day Tracking

Evening Reading:

Meditate ☐
(pg 659)

SATURDAY — MORNING PREPARATION
WEEK 12, DAY 7

DATE:

How long did you sleep?   Meditate ☐   Morning Reading:
(pg 658)

How well did you sleep? /5   Exercise ☐

NOTES:

Review your 7-day goals. With those goals in mind, make a **'Knockout List'** of 3-5 tasks you must work to complete today. Specify the tasks, and make them something you expect you can achieve today.

What are some obstacles you are likely to face today?

What can you do to prepare for or reduce the chances of them happening?

What should you do if these obstacles happen?

> "You don't develop courage by being happy in your relationships everyday. You develop it by surviving difficult times and challenging adversity."
>
> - *Epictetus*

(See pg 656 for writing prompts)

EVENING REVIEW

BREAKFAST	LUNCH	SUPPER	SNACKS

What were the most significant obstacles you faced today?

How could these obstacles have been worse?

How did you or how can you mitigate these obstacles?

How can you reduce the chances of them reoccurring?

How can these obstacles benefit you?

What mistakes did you make today?

What could you have done that would have been worse?

What can you do to mitigate these mistakes?

What could you do better next time?

What did you do well today?

What can you look forward to tomorrow?

Did you do what was appropriate to complete your tasks?	**YES / NO**
Did you complete your knockout list?	**YES / NO**
Are you closer to your goals today?	**YES / NO**
Did you behave according to your principles?	**YES / NO**

◯ Fill in your Gratitude Log and 28 Day Tracking

Evening Reading:

Meditate ☐
(pg 659)

WEEK 12 GRATITUDE LOG

Write briefly about anything that you have to be grateful for for each day.

If you are having difficulty thinking about what to write, you can consult the prompts on page 657.

SUNDAY

MONDAY

TUESDAY

WEDNESDAY

THURSDAY

FRIDAY

SATURDAY

WEEKLY PREMEDITATION OF OBSTACLES

Think of a significant obstacle happening to you, or think about suffering a significant loss. Imagine it as if it were happening now. Describe it in detail.

What would be the best way to react to this happening?

What are some things you now enjoy which you could no longer enjoy if this happens to you? Describe what you enjoy about it in detail.

How could you repair any damage caused if this happened?

What could you still enjoy in your life if this happened?

What could you do to prepare for or reduce the chances of this happening?

It's a possibility that this could happen to you. But it hasn't yet. What can you do to appreciate what you have now?

28 DAY TRACKING - WEEKS 9-12

WEEK 12 REVIEW

○ Review your 7-day goals. Did you accomplish them? **YES / NO**
If no, consider why not, and if it is still worth your time. If it is, migrate it forward into a future task.

What were the best things that happened this week?

Which activities did not work well for you this week?

What activities worked well for you this week?

Overall, this week was:

7-DAY GOAL SETTING - WEEK 13

Review your 35 day goals. Consider the steps you should do to achieve the goals, and what you can do to reduce the chances of the obstacles you anticipated. With those in mind, what are your goals for the next 7 days? Make them specific and achievable in 7 days.

Why are these steps important?

What part of these steps are in your control?

WEEKLY THEME

Build Community

WEEKLY REFLECTION

(See pg 656 for writing prompts)

609

WEEK 13 PLANNER

	SUNDAY	MONDAY	TUESDAY

	WEDNESDAY	THURSDAY	FRIDAY	SATURDAY

SUNDAY — MORNING PREPARATION
WEEK 13, DAY 1

DATE:

How long did you sleep? Meditate ☐
(pg 658)

How well did you sleep? /5 Exercise ☐

Morning Reading:

NOTES:

Review your 7-day goals. With those goals in mind, make a **'Knockout List'** of 3-5 tasks you must work to complete today. Specify the tasks, and make them something you expect you can achieve today.

What are some obstacles you are likely to face today?

What can you do to prepare for or reduce the chances of them happening?

What should you do if these obstacles happen?

"Ponder for a long time whether you shall admit a given person to your friendship; but when you have decided to admit him, welcome him with all your heart and soul."

- Seneca

(See pg 656 for writing prompts)

EVENING REVIEW

BREAKFAST	LUNCH	SUPPER	SNACKS

What were the most significant obstacles you faced today?

How could these obstacles have been worse?

How did you or how can you mitigate these obstacles?

How can you reduce the chances of them reoccurring?

How can these obstacles benefit you?

What mistakes did you make today?

What could you have done that would have been worse?

What can you do to mitigate these mistakes?

What could you do better next time?

What did you do well today?

What can you look forward to tomorrow?

Did you do what was appropriate to complete your tasks?	**YES / NO**
Did you complete your knockout list?	**YES / NO**
Are you closer to your goals today?	**YES / NO**
Did you behave according to your principles?	**YES / NO**

Fill in your Gratitude Log and 7 Day Tracking

Evening Reading:

Meditate ☐
(pg 659)

MONDAY
MORNING PREPARATION
WEEK 13, DAY 2

DATE:

How long did you sleep?   Meditate ☐
(pg 658)

How well did you sleep? /5   Exercise ☐

Morning Reading:

NOTES:

Review your 7-day goals. With those goals in mind, make a **'Knockout List'** of 3-5 tasks you must work to complete today. Specify the tasks, and make them something you expect you can achieve today.

What are some obstacles you are likely to face today?

What can you do to prepare for or reduce the chances of them happening?

What should you do if these obstacles happen?

> "We Stoics ... take pleasure in bestowing benefits, even though they cost us labour, provided that they lighten the labours of others."
>
> *- Seneca*

(See pg 656 for writing prompts)

EVENING REVIEW

BREAKFAST	LUNCH	SUPPER	SNACKS

What were the most significant obstacles you faced today?

How could these obstacles have been worse?

How did you or how can you mitigate these obstacles?

How can you reduce the chances of them reoccurring?

How can these obstacles benefit you?

What mistakes did you make today?

What could you have done that would have been worse?

What can you do to mitigate these mistakes?

What could you do better next time?

What did you do well today?

What can you look forward to tomorrow?

Did you do what was appropriate to complete your tasks?	**YES / NO**
Did you complete your knockout list?	**YES / NO**
Are you closer to your goals today?	**YES / NO**
Did you behave according to your principles?	**YES / NO**

◯ Fill in your Gratitude Log and 7 Day Tracking

Evening Reading:

Meditate ☐
(pg 659)

TUESDAY — MORNING PREPARATION
WEEK 13, DAY 3

DATE:

How long did you sleep? Meditate ☐   Morning Reading:
(pg 658)

How well did you sleep? /5   Exercise ☐

NOTES:

Review your 7-day goals. With those goals in mind, make a **'Knockout List'** of 3-5 tasks you must work to complete today. Specify the tasks, and make them something you expect you can achieve today.

What are some obstacles you are likely to face today?

What can you do to prepare for or reduce the chances of them happening?

What should you do if these obstacles happen?

"There is a standard of righteousness that might does not make right, that the end does not justify the means, and that expediency as a working principle is bound to fail. The only hope of perfecting human relationships is in accordance with the law of service under which men are not so solicitous about what they shall get as they are about what they shall give. Yet people are entitled to the rewards of their industry. What they earn is theirs, no matter how small or how great. But the possession of property carries the obligation to use it in a larger service."

- Calvin Coolidge

(See pg 656 for writing prompts)

EVENING REVIEW

BREAKFAST	LUNCH	SUPPER	SNACKS

What were the most significant obstacles you faced today?

How could these obstacles have been worse?

How did you or how can you mitigate these obstacles?

How can you reduce the chances of them reoccurring?

How can these obstacles benefit you?

What mistakes did you make today?

What could you have done that would have been worse?

What can you do to mitigate these mistakes?

What could you do better next time?

What did you do well today?

What can you look forward to tomorrow?

Did you do what was appropriate to complete your tasks?	**YES / NO**
Did you complete your knockout list?	**YES / NO**
Are you closer to your goals today?	**YES / NO**
Did you behave according to your principles?	**YES / NO**

Fill in your Gratitude Log and 7 Day Tracking

Evening Reading:

Meditate ☐
(pg 659)

WEDNESDAY — WEEK 13, DAY 4
MORNING PREPARATION

DATE:

How long did you sleep? Meditate ☐
(pg 658)

How well did you sleep? /5 Exercise ☐

Morning Reading:

NOTES:

Review your 7-day goals. With those goals in mind, make a **'Knockout List'** of 3-5 tasks you must work to complete today. Specify the tasks, and make them something you expect you can achieve today.

What are some obstacles you are likely to face today?

What can you do to prepare for or reduce the chances of them happening?

What should you do if these obstacles happen?

> "Let your impulse to act and your action have as their goal the service of the human community, because that, for you, is in conformity with your nature."
>
> *- Marcus Aurelius*

(See pg 656 for writing prompts)

EVENING REVIEW

BREAKFAST	LUNCH	SUPPER	SNACKS

What were the most significant obstacles you faced today?

How could these obstacles have been worse?

How did you or how can you mitigate these obstacles?

How can you reduce the chances of them reoccurring?

How can these obstacles benefit you?

What mistakes did you make today?

What could you have done that would have been worse?

What can you do to mitigate these mistakes?

What could you do better next time?

What did you do well today?

What can you look forward to tomorrow?

Did you do what was appropriate to complete your tasks?	**YES / NO**
Did you complete your knockout list?	**YES / NO**
Are you closer to your goals today?	**YES / NO**
Did you behave according to your principles?	**YES / NO**

Fill in your Gratitude Log and 7 Day Tracking

Evening Reading:

Meditate ☐
(pg 659)

THURSDAY — WEEK 13, DAY 5
MORNING PREPARATION

DATE:

How long did you sleep?　　Meditate ☐　　Morning Reading:
(pg 658)

How well did you sleep?　/5　Exercise ☐

NOTES:

Review your 7-day goals. With those goals in mind, make a **'Knockout List'** of 3-5 tasks you must work to complete today. Specify the tasks, and make them something you expect you can achieve today.

What are some obstacles you are likely to face today?

What can you do to prepare for or reduce the chances of them happening?

What should you do if these obstacles happen?

> "We like to say that we don't get to choose our parents, that they were given by chance—yet we can truly choose whose children we'd like to be."
>
> *- Seneca*

(See pg 656 for writing prompts)

EVENING REVIEW

BREAKFAST	LUNCH	SUPPER	SNACKS

What were the most significant obstacles you faced today?

How could these obstacles have been worse?

How did you or how can you mitigate these obstacles?

How can you reduce the chances of them reoccurring?

How can these obstacles benefit you?

What mistakes did you make today?

What could you have done that would have been worse?

What can you do to mitigate these mistakes?

What could you do better next time?

What did you do well today?

What can you look forward to tomorrow?

Did you do what was appropriate to complete your tasks?	**YES / NO**
Did you complete your knockout list?	**YES / NO**
Are you closer to your goals today?	**YES / NO**
Did you behave according to your principles?	**YES / NO**

Fill in your Gratitude Log and 7 Day Tracking

Evening Reading:

Meditate ☐
(pg 659)

FRIDAY
MORNING PREPARATION
WEEK 13, DAY 6

DATE:

How long did you sleep? Meditate ☐
(pg 658)

How well did you sleep? /5 Exercise ☐

Morning Reading:

NOTES:

Review your 7-day goals. With those goals in mind, make a **'Knockout List'** of 3-5 tasks you must work to complete today. Specify the tasks, and make them something you expect you can achieve today.

What are some obstacles you are likely to face today?

What can you do to prepare for or reduce the chances of them happening?

What should you do if these obstacles happen?

> "Games also will be useful: for moderate pleasure relieves the mind and brings it to a proper balance"
>
> *- Seneca*

(See pg 656 for writing prompts)

EVENING REVIEW

BREAKFAST	LUNCH	SUPPER	SNACKS

What were the most significant obstacles you faced today?

How could these obstacles have been worse?

How did you or how can you mitigate these obstacles?

How can you reduce the chances of them reoccurring?

How can these obstacles benefit you?

What mistakes did you make today?

What could you have done that would have been worse?

What can you do to mitigate these mistakes?

What could you do better next time?

What did you do well today?

What can you look forward to tomorrow?

Did you do what was appropriate to complete your tasks?	**YES / NO**
Did you complete your knockout list?	**YES / NO**
Are you closer to your goals today?	**YES / NO**
Did you behave according to your principles?	**YES / NO**

○ Fill in your Gratitude Log and 7 Day Tracking

Evening Reading:

Meditate ☐
(pg 659)

SATURDAY — MORNING PREPARATION
WEEK 13, DAY 7

DATE:

How long did you sleep? Meditate ☐ (pg 658)

How well did you sleep? /5 Exercise ☐

Morning Reading:

NOTES:

Review your 7-day goals. With those goals in mind, make a **'Knockout List'** of 3-5 tasks you must work to complete today. Specify the tasks, and make them something you expect you can achieve today.

What are some obstacles you are likely to face today?

What can you do to prepare for or reduce the chances of them happening?

What should you do if these obstacles happen?

"Nothing will ever please me, no matter how excellent or beneficial, if I must retain the knowledge of it to myself. And if wisdom were given to me under the express condition that it must be kept hidden and not uttered, I should refuse it. No good thing is pleasant to possess, without friends to share it."

- Seneca

(See pg 656 for writing prompts)

EVENING REVIEW

BREAKFAST	LUNCH	SUPPER	SNACKS

What were the most significant obstacles you faced today?

How could these obstacles have been worse?

How did you or how can you mitigate these obstacles?

How can you reduce the chances of them reoccurring?

How can these obstacles benefit you?

What mistakes did you make today?

What could you have done that would have been worse?

What can you do to mitigate these mistakes?

What could you do better next time?

What did you do well today?

What can you look forward to tomorrow?

Did you do what was appropriate to complete your tasks?	**YES / NO**
Did you complete your knockout list?	**YES / NO**
Are you closer to your goals today?	**YES / NO**
Did you behave according to your principles?	**YES / NO**

Fill in your Gratitude Log and 28 Day Tracking

Evening Reading:

Meditate ☐
(pg 659)

WEEK 13 GRATITUDE LOG

Write briefly about anything that you have to be grateful for for each day.

If you are having difficulty thinking about what to write, you can consult the prompts on page 657.

SUNDAY

MONDAY

TUESDAY

WEDNESDAY

THURSDAY

FRIDAY

SATURDAY

WEEKLY PREMEDITATION OF OBSTACLES

Think of a significant obstacle happening to you, or think about suffering a significant loss. Imagine it as if it were happening now. Describe it in detail.

What would be the best way to react to this happening?

What are some things you now enjoy which you could no longer enjoy if this happens to you? Describe what you enjoy about it in detail.

How could you repair any damage caused if this happened?

What could you still enjoy in your life if this happened?

What could you do to prepare for or reduce the chances of this happening?

It's a possibility that this could happen to you. But it hasn't yet. What can you do to appreciate what you have now?

7 DAY TRACKING - WEEK 13

Week 13

HEALTH & WELLNESS REVIEW - WEEKS 9-13

	CURRENT	CHANGE	TARGET
Weight			
Body Fat %			
Neck			
Shoulders			
Chest			
Right Bicep			
Left Bicep			
Right Forearm			
Left Forearm			
Waist			
Hips			
Right Thigh			
Left Thigh			
Right Calf			
Left Calf			
Push-ups in 60 seconds			
Pull-ups in 60 seconds/Flex Arm Hang			
Squats in 60 seconds			
Sit-ups in 60 seconds			
Sit & Reach Distance			
Heartbeat after 3 Min Stair Climb			

On average for the last 5 weeks, how much do you agree?
On a scale of 1-10 with 1 being least agreement and 10 being most agreement

		CURRENT	CHANGE
PHYSICAL HEALTH	I am clean and orderly		
	I am sleeping well		
	I am exercising well		
	I feel properly energetic		
	Total Physical Health Score:		
EMOTIONAL HEALTH	I am not feeling worried or anxious		
	I am able to relax		
	I feel a sense of tranquility		
	I am not easily annoyed or irritated		
	Total Emotional Health Score:		
INTELLECTUAL HEALTH	I am consistently learning		
	I can consider ideas that I disagree with		
	I can change my opinion when appropriate		
	I am intellectually challenged		
	Total Intellectual Health Score:		
SPIRITUAL HEALTH	I can forgive myself and others		
	I feel a strong purpose in my life		
	I accept what I cannot change		
	I practice routines to develop my spirit		
	Total Spiritual Health Score:		
SOCIAL HEALTH	I don't feel lonely		
	I enjoy spending time with others		
	I make a positive contribution to my community		
	I do not attempt to avoid people		
	Total Social Health Score:		

Total Score:		Change:	

WEEK 13 REVIEW

○ Review your 7-day goals. Did you accomplish them? **YES / NO** If no, consider why not, and if it is still worth your time. If it is, migrate it forward into a future task.

What were the best things that happened this week?

Which activities did not work well for you this week?

What activities worked well for you this week?

Overall, this week was:

35 DAY REVIEW

◯ Review your 35-day goals. Did you accomplish them? **YES / NO**
If no, consider why not, and if it is still worth your time. If it is, migrate it forward into a future task.

What were the best things that happened these last four weeks?

Which activities did not work well for you these last four weeks?

What activities worked well for you these last four weeks?

QUARTERLY REVIEW

Congratulations!

You've completed this quarter.

○ Review your quarterly goals. Did you accomplish them? **YES / NO**

If you acomplished your quarterly goals, **congratulations** again! If not, did your plan turn out to be appropriate for the goal? **YES / NO**
If not, what could you change about the plan to better succeed?

If your plan was appropriate, did you have the right execution of the steps? If not, what could you change in your actions to better succeed?

If you both had the right plan and actions, but still didn't meet the goal, what could you change to improve your ability to succeed?

> If you did not accomplish your goals, consider if the goals are still worth your time. If they are, migrate them forward into a future task.

What are some aspects you enjoyed on this journey?

Keep up the momentum! What should you do next?

Ok, you know what to do next. Now go do it!

Writing Prompts

Here are some prompts on what you can reflect upon for the weekly theme or the day's thought. You can answer as many or as few of these questions as you find beneficial.

- What does this concept mean to you?
- How have you seen this concept in the past?
- How would living in accord with this concept benefit you?
- How would living in accord with this concept benefit your community?
- How has your life reflected this concept?
- How has your life contradicted this concept?
- Who is someone you know or know of that has exemplified this concept and how?
- How could your life reflect this concept better going forward?

- For the daily thought, how does this quote relate to the weekly reflection?

Gratitude Prompts

If you are having difficulty thinking of what you have to be grateful for on any given day, here are some topics that you can think of for your gratitude. If you feel that none of these are appropriate for today, you can also be grateful for having had these in the past.

- Your favourite moment of the day
- The good qualities in a person you know or know of
- A random act of kindness from you or another person
- Something that cheers you up
- A success you had
- A favourite hobby
- Something good in your work or personal life
- Something you accomplished
- Something someone else did that you liked
- Something you did to help another person
- Something about a pet or other animal that you like
- Something you like about yourself.
- Something you think is beautiful
- A favourite memory
- Opportunities you have
- Something you treasure
- A person or people you love
- Something about the current season
- A book you enjoyed
- Good news
- The biggest gift in your life now or in the past
- How you have grown in life

If you continue to have difficulty, you can also reference the gratitude meditation on page 662 for ideas on what else you can be grateful for.

MORNING MEDITATION

Do each of the following meditations in this order:

1 - Zazen Breathing Meditation (pg 660)

2 - Panta Rhei Meditation (pg 661)

>Read, say, or listen to the meditation in the box once.

3 - Gratitude Meditation (pg 662)

>Read, say, or listen to the meditation in the box once.

4 - Adversity Meditation (pg 663)

>Read, say, or listen to the meditation in the box once.

5 - Agape Meditation (pg 665)

>Read, say, or listen to the meditation in the first box once, and in the second box four times - once for each person or group of people you are thinking of as instructed.

EVENING MEDITATION

Do each of the following meditations in this order:

1 - Zazen Breathing Meditation (pg 660)

2 - Panta Rhei Meditation (pg 661)

    Read, say, or listen to the meditation in the box once.

3 - Gratitude Meditation (pg 662)

    Read, say, or listen to the meditation in the box once.

4 - Forgiveness Meditation (pg 664)

    Read, say, or listen to the meditation in the box once.

5 - Agape Meditation (pg 665)

    Read, say, or listen to the meditation in the first box once, and in the second box four times - once for each person or group of people you are thinking of as instructed.

ZAZEN MEDITATION

Two to Seven Minutes of Zazen Breathing Meditation

Have a few minutes of quiet sitting to clear your mind of distractions.

Assume a comfortable seated position and keep your back straight.

Hold your head in a comfortable position, with your head aligned with your straight back, and your chin tucked in slightly.

Focus your eyes just ahead of you, either at a wall or at the floor. Keep your eyes slightly closed

Try not to think of anything at all, except perhaps your breath.

Try to expand your belly more than your chest as you breathe in through your nose.

Hold your breath slightly and only without any strain.

Breathe out through your nose.

Pay attention to rhythm and sound of your breathing. Feel the air entering and exiting your lungs. Strive to be as aware as possible of your breathing for the duration of your meditation.

If you start to think of anything other than your breath, bring your thoughts back to focus on your breath alone. If this is difficult, you can count your breaths until you no longer need to in order to keep your thoughts on your breath.

When learning Zazen, start with a 2 minute session. Increase that duration as your skill increases. A 7 minute session should be sufficient to clear your thoughts for the rest of your Stoic meditation.

PANTA RHEI MEDITATION

Everything Flows.

Consider how the things in your life are imperfect, impermanent, and incomplete. See the beauty in this.

Nothing ever is, everything is becoming. All things are in motion like streams. All things are passing, and nothing abides.

Everything and everyone is imperfect. I have flaws and imperfections, as does everyone else. This is part of what we are and what makes us unique. There is beauty in the imperfections.

Everything and everyone is impermanent. Nothing stays the same. Nothing lasts forever. Change is the only constant. There is nothing we can really hold on to. These moments will never happen again. There is beauty in the impermanence.

Everything and everyone is incomplete. The world is a work in progress. You are a work in progress. There is beauty in this process of becoming.

GRATITUDE MEDITATION

No day is guaranteed to me. But today I am alive and air fills my lungs. For this, I am grateful.

I have consciousness. I have reason. For this, I am grateful.

I know very little, but I am not finished learning. For this, I am grateful.

I am not perfect, but I am not finished growing. For this, I am grateful.

My past is gone. I can start life anew today. For this, I am grateful.

I have the capacity to be virtuous, and virtue is sufficient for happiness. For this, I am grateful.

I don't need anything outside of myself to be content. For this, I am grateful.

I am able to be good. I am able to love. For this, I am grateful.

It is in my power to be free and at peace. For this, I am grateful.

I cannot control what happens to me. But I can control how I react. For this, I am grateful.

With every trial, I am able to learn a lesson. For this, I am grateful.

With every hardship, I am able to respond with good. For this, I am grateful.

I can choose to forgive. For this, I am grateful.

The universe follows an order. Everything happens as it should. For this, I am grateful.

Everything is interwoven. I am a part of the divine. For this, I am grateful.

I am the universe, living briefly as a human. For this, I am grateful.

I will return to the universe and live on as it does. For this, I am grateful.

ADVERSITY MEDITATION

Remember, today you will face adversity

People I deal with today will be meddling, ungrateful, arrogant, dishonest, malicious, bitter, resentful, vindictive, jealous, and surly. They are like this because they confuse good and evil.

But I have seen the beauty of good, and the ugliness of evil, and have recognized that the wrongdoer has a nature kindred to my own - not of the same blood and birth, but the same mind, the same humanity, and possessing a share of the divine.

No wrongdoer can harm me. No one can bring me into evil. Nor can I feel angry at my kindred, or hate them. We were born to work together like feet, hands and eyes, like the two rows of teeth, upper and lower. To obstruct each other is deviant. To feel anger at someone, to turn your back on him: these are deviant.

FORGIVENESS MEDITATION

Forgive yourself and others for mistakes

Remember that we are all a product of the sum of our experiences. If you had all the same circumstances of birth and life happen to as those who harmed you, then you would have also acted as they did.

Remember that no one does evil knowingly or willingly. We do wrong when we are confused about the true nature of what is good.

Say the following in your meditation on forgiveness:

> If I have failed or harmed anyone in any way either knowingly or unknowingly, it was due to my own confusions; I ask their forgiveness.
>
> If anyone has failed or harmed me in any way either knowingly or unknowingly, it was due to their own confusions; I forgive them.
>
> For all the ways that I fail or harm myself, negate, doubt, belittle myself, judge or be unkind to myself, and for all the ways I fail to act according to my own principles, it is due to my own confusions; I forgive myself.
>
> And if there is a situation I am not yet ready to forgive, it is due to my own confusions; I forgive myself for that.

AGAPE MEDITATION

A meditation for an unconditional, cosmopolitan love for all.

In this meditation you will wish well for yourself, and wish for others as you wish for yourself.

- **Love yourself.** Think of yourself and say:

> I am important. I matter. I am precious. I am good.
>
> May I be at peace. May I be content and of a good spirit.
>
> May I be free and prosperous.
>
> May I want for nothing, suffer no misfortune, and live a good life.

- **Love your family and friends.** Now imagine your friends and family, and say for them:

> You are important. You matter. You are precious. You are good.
>
> May you be at peace. May you be content and of a good spirit.
>
> May you be free and prosperous.
>
> May you want for nothing, suffer no misfortune, and live a good life.

- **Love your neighbours.** Think of someone you know who is not a friend or family, and say the same for them.

- **Love your enemies.** Think of someone who has done you wrong, or dislikes you, or even wishes you harm, and say the same for them.

- **Love all of mankind.** Imagine the people you haven't met - all of humanity - and say the same for them.

The Focused Stoic Journal / 91 Day Undated Edition by Jeff Rout

Published by Domino Effect Publishing

© 2020 Jeff Rout

All rights reserved. No portion of this book may be reproduced in any form without permission from the publisher, except as permitted by Canadian and/or U.S. copyright law.

Cover by Jeff Rout

ISBN: 978-0-9867593-8-3

www.ingramcontent.com/pod-product-compliance
Lightning Source LLC
Chambersburg PA
CBHW032020290426

44110CB00012B/611